TWO FACES OF ISLAM

Birth of Islam
And
Creation of the Empire

Looking at Islam from a new viewpoint

ISBN: 0-9717177-1-0

**Published in the
United States of America
By**

**New Horizons
P.O. Box 896
Glendale, CA 91206**
www.cfiwest.org/newhorizons
e-mail: Armen@cfiwest.org
January 2002

Table of Content

Headings   **Page**

Acknowledgements

I wish to take this opportunity to express my heartfelt thanks to Dr. Paul Kurtz for his trust in me and the leadership he has provided. I would also like to express my sincere thanks to a dear friend, Mr. Ranjit Sandhu, who took the time to make my written English readable. Also my thanks to another dear friend Mr. Mohammad Shahdadi who took the time to read all of the names of the people, places and references, one by one, and made valuable corrections and suggestions in their correct spellings.

Above all, I would like to express my gratitude to two other dear persons. First my son, Arthur George Saginian, who literally forced himself to read the published book and told me that my English is bad, I have many mistakes, and advised me to seek editorial help. Secondly, my thanks to a dear friend, Professor Emeritus of English and ex-dean of Maryville College, Dr. Arthur S. Bushing who was persuaded to take the time and make this book readable.

In this second edition, that combines the book1 and book 2 of the previously published *"Two Faces of Islam"*, I would like to acknowledge the comments of many readers who encouraged and persuaded me to combine these two booklets into one. Previous publications were in smaller size and in saddle-stitched form with no spine. Most booksellers and distributors, whether chain store or independent shopkeepers, refused to accept and sell books that, due to lack of spine, could not be placed on the bookshelves and put of display.

BOOK 1

**Life of Mohammad
Beginning of Islam**

Introduction

The American public, in general, knows little about Islam. Any judgment passed or any conclusion reached by any member of the public or its leaders with little or no factual information on the matter is bound to be erroneous.

Here at New Horizons, it is our intention to introduce Islam to you, the American public, in a readable language, at an affordable price, and in the smallest digest form possible. This book and the others that will follow are pocket-size, designed to fit in any pocket or purse. Each of these books costs about the price of a pack of cigarettes and contains more information than most hard-cover editions.

Why are we publishing this book you may ask. Because, for the first time in the history of the United States, its citizens are going to interact with something that is not what they think it is.

Most Americans are religious, mostly Christian, and think of Islam as just another religion. It is not. Islam is an integrated conglomeration of religion, government, and law. In other words, it is an *Ideology*. When Islam is referred to as a religion, and Muslims are thought of as people who adhere to that religion, a misconception is formed that could well cause major problems for us as a sovereign nation.

Libraries have thousands of books on Islam. Most are scholarly works that are read only by scholars. Some are works of apologetics (written from an Islamic point of view, defending Islam). These serve to misguide the reader. Some books address only a particular aspect of the subject. Further, most of the American public is uninformed about their contents, even as biased as they may be.

The events of September 11th, 2001, have changed our lives and have forced us, the American public, to deal with Muslims. Consequently we should know them, understand them, recognize their **modus operendi,** and be prepared to face them on their own grounds. Unlike us, they have their own laws, laws that come from Allah (God), laws that are thus unchangeable and negotiable. Muslims live and die by them.

Americans is right from the beginning. Islam began with Mohammad, but now it is not what it was under him. Mohammad accomplished the goal he had set for himself. Others came later and set their own goals. The net result was that an empire was created that now commands over one billion mental-slaves and is sustained by their servitude.

Please note that this book is neither a history text nor the result of a new research on Islam and Mohammad. It is only an overview and review of events that took place over fourteen centuries ago. It is just a report on observation of a total stranger, like a visitor from outer space who knows nothing about what has been going on in that region before and after Mohammad and is detached from the people living there. All the information herein has been extracted from the writings of Mohammad's contemporaries. Most of them are from Arabic sources, and the rest from the writings of non-Arab observers who were living there at the time. Nothing has been changed or altered in any way or manner. It is being presented in as digested a form as possible. All the non-action information has been expunged from this presentation; otherwise, it would have filled several volumes.

Who Was Mohammad?

One of the most populous and powerful tribes of Arabia was, and still is, the Ghoreysh, and people of that tribe are referred to as Ghoreyshi. Bani-Hashem and Bani-Omayye are two clans of Ghoreysh. Mohammad's father Abdollah, and his mother, Ameneh, were born into the Bani-Hashem clan of the Ghoreysh tribe. Mohammad was born in Mecca on Monday, the 12th day of Rabi-ol-avval, which some say is 572 A.D., but according to the **Encyclopedia Britannica** it is 570 A.D.

Abdollah died of illness before his son Mohammad was born. The only material goods he left for his wife and son were five camels and one slave named Om-Imen (mother of Imen). Mohammad's mother,Ameneh, was sickly and unable to care for her son. Thus she gave him over to Halimeh Khatoon, a member of the Bani-Saad tribe, to be nursed and taken care of.

Mohammad stayed with Halimeh until he was five years old. In this time he saw his mother twice. He was two years old at the time of the first visit and four at the second. A few months later she passed away, leaving him an orphan.

After Ameneh's death, Mohammad was turned over to his paternal grandfather, Abd-ol-Motleb, who was 108 years old. Mohammad stayed with him until his death three years later. At the age of nine Mohammad went to live with his paternal uncle, Abu-Taleb.

Having been in the custody of various people at such an early age of his life surely had a permanent effect upon him emotionally. In addition, he was epileptic. It was primarily for this reason that Halimeh returned him to his mother Ameneh. The effect of being handed over from one custodian to another is reflected in the Koran (Chapter 93, Verses 5-9):

وَلَسَوْفَ يُعْطِيكَ رَبُّكَ فَتَرْضَى ﴿٥﴾   أَلَمْ يَجِدْكَ يَتِيمًا فَآوَى ﴿٦﴾

وَوَجَدَكَ ضَالًّا فَهَدَى ﴿٧﴾   وَوَجَدَكَ عَآئِلاً فَأَغْنَى ﴿٨﴾   فَأَمَّا الْيَتِيمَ فَلَا تَقْهَرْ ﴿٩﴾

"Did We not find you orphaned and housed you? Were you not lost and We guided you? Were you not in need of family and help, and We fulfilled your need? Don't shun the orphan and don't cause pain to the beggar".

Thus began Mohammad's education in the school of life. We should note that although epileptic, Mohammad was strongly built and very bright. We shall follow the development of his character throughout his life.

His uncle, Abu-Taleb, employed him to tend his camels. The growing bright, young man, in the middle of the empty and harsh desert, began to think, analyze, and make decisions.

Abu-Taleb concluded that Mohammad was old enough to tend the camels in his caravans. Thus

Mohammad began to travel to Damascus. He made this trip several times between the ages of 10 to 14. Distance from Mecca to Damascus is about 1,000 miles; traveling with a caravan, this would take over 50 days. In those days caravans would lodge for the night. The lodgings were not necessarily covered buildings, but were safe nevertheless. They were located at crossroads. There were such lodgings in Iran as well, and in Farsi language they were called Carvansaray, which leterally means "hall of caravans." In Arabic they were called Rabat. Caravans from various places and traveling to various destinations would gather around to pass the night. They found safety in numbers.

Consider the wagon trains of the old west as a similar case in point. Replace the Indians with caravan robbers, replace the horses and oxen with camels, guns with swords and spears. And instead of wagon trains, imagine lines of loaded camels. In the old Arabia, just as in the old west, caravans settled down at the lodgings and formed corrals in a defensive circle.

The caravanners would light fires, eat evening meals, talk, and sleep. These caravan lodges became Mohammad's information school. He began to learn from various clerics about their religions. At that time, there were Jewish rabbis, Christian priests, and Zoroastrian moghs or moubeds. He must have found it fascinating that people of the cloth could make a very good living by traveling and talking. It was indeed a most interesting life. One carries nothing but words, does nothing but talk, has nothing to be robbed or killed for, but, most important of all, commands respect from his audience and is cared for.

He decided to learn the trade.

Upon his return from his last trip to Damascus, he found his home town under attack by Nexus Abraheh, Governor of Abyssinia, who had decided to destroy Mecca and to make Sanaa the new trading center. Because his army was riding on elephants, Arabs called his starting point Om-ol-Fil (Fil means elephant). Mohammad was thought to have participated in that war. He deserted and became the laughing stock of his acquaintances and friends. The ridicule forced him to leave his uncle's home and to leave Mecca. He was 25 years old.

To survive, he became a shepherd. It is interesting to note that most, if not all, of those who have claimed to be prophets or messengers of God had, at one time or another, been a shepherd. This may suggest that there must be a similarity between the basic character of crowds on the one hand and herds of sheep or goats on the other. At any rate, in those days, being a shepherd was the lowest form of occupation that a 25-year-old man could have in Arabia.

After working as a shepherd, Mohammad was hired in the southern part of Mecca by a clothing merchant named Saeb. It was in this establishment that he met Khadijeh, a widow who had outlived three previous husbands. She had wealth and a good social status. About her wealth – if we can accept everything that we read – it is written that she had over 80,000 camels. Simply feeding that many camels requires an immense amount of feed and water. Not every Tom or Joe could handle such an expense. Assuming the number to be true, where could one get all that feed and water in the Arabian desert?

Khadijeh was a merchant, and her caravans carried her goods among Egypt, Abyssinia, Damascus, and Mecca. In Mohammad she saw a tall, strong, handsome, masculine, and honest visionary. And Khadijeh had visions of her own as well. Arrangements were made and they married.

Thanks to his wife, Mohammad now became a man of wealth. Seeing the pathetic financial situation of his uncle, Abu-Taleb, he brought his cousin Ali to live with them. With his wife's wealth at his disposal, he became benevolent and helped many people. Khadijeh gave birth to two boys and four girls. Both boys died in their infancy, but the girls survived. Mohammad's first son was named Qassem, and for that reason, according to Arabic customs, Mohammad is sometimes referred to as Abu-al-Qassem, which means "father of Qassem."

Mohammad's most comfortable years were from the age of 35 to 40. It was this comfort that allowed him other ventures. He was solitary, and he usually took solitude in the Cave of Harra. That was where he meditated. He kept away from people, and it is a puzzle how such a solitary man, who shied away from multitudes, could proclaim himself a prophet. It is said that exposure to people reminded him of his painful past as an orphan child and as a poor and destitute man who could not feed himself.

Mohammad frequented the cave more often. Every year he spent the entire month of Ramazan (Ramadan) there. There are many tales as to what took place in that cave. After several years, at the age of forty, he declared that the Archangel Gabriel had appeared to him and ordered him to read. This is accepted as a miracle. But if he did not know how to read and write (as the Islamic apologists claim), how could he have kept records of his trading first for his uncle and later for Khadijeh? At the same time that Mohammad announced that Gabriel had visited him, he also declared that Allah (God) had appointed him to be His Messenger.

Who Is Allah?

In the central Mosque of Mecca, there is a large black stone known as the Hajar-al-Aswad ("Black stone"). It had been stored in a cubicle known as Kaaba. This had been a place of worship for the Arabs for centuries, long before the appearance of Mohammad. Various Arab tribes who had stored their idols would come to worship and pay homage. This pilgrimage took place once a year, and that period of visitation was known as Hajj. Mohammad made Hajj one of the five obligatory requirements for each and every Muslim.

Many researchers have looked into the origin of the name Allah. There are twenty theories concerning its origin. What is clear is that the name Allah did exist long before Mohammad was born. Mohammad's father was named Abdollah, which means "slave of Allah." That was the name he received at birth, and he was rather old when he sired Mohammad. Slaves were seldom named after their masters – such a name was usually given as an honorary tribute to a deity. The house of Kaaba was called Beitollah centuries before Mohammad. In Arabic this means "the house of Allah." Since only idols were housed there, it follows that Allah must have been one of the idols, and an important one at that. Pre-Islamic literature indicates that the worshipers who visited Kaaba, in their prayer ceremony, would raise their arms and chant, "O Allah, we have come to worship you."

Approximately 360 idols were stored in Kaaba.

The most revered idol of the Ghoreysh was Azzi. There were three other great idols - Lot, Manat and Allah. Allah was the greatest idol, and Mohammad chose him to be the one and only God of all Muslims.

Mohammad the Preacher

As mentioned, Mohammad belonged to the clan of Bani-Hashem, one of many clans of the Ghoreysh tribe. Traditionally the Kaaba was in the custody of the strongest tribe. In Mohammad's time, the Ghoreysh tribe had the privilege. As such, they received payments from other tribes for services rendered in caring for their idols. Mohammad began to preach Islam, and this was unacceptable to both his clansmen and his tribe. It was paradoxical how a member of a tribe that housed idols could preach monotheism. Monotheism would deprive the tribe of its income, as no service would be required for the idols. Mohammad was warned to stop his preaching.

He did not stop, and the threats became serious. Thirteen years of preaching had accomplished little. All he had to show for his efforts was a handful of converts. Among them were his cousin Ali, his wife Khadijeh, his freed slave Zayd, his friend Abu Bakr, and a few others. Nonetheless the Ghoreysh were adamantly opposed to his efforts. His paternal uncle Abu-Taleb asked him to stop the nonsense, but Mohammad shed tears and refused to quit.

Disappointed in the Ghoreysh, Mohammad decided to go after the people of Yasreb. He thought they were better candidates for Islam: first, because they had been exposed to Jewish teaching and had heard that Jews believed a Savior would come to save them; and second, because they had a longstanding animosity toward the people of Mecca. The heads of Ghoreysh would take no more, and the pleas of Abu-Taleb now fell on deaf ears.

Mohammad was exiled from Mecca. He stayed near Mecca, though, preaching to caravanners, until Abu-Taleb managed to reverse the sentence. Mohammad returned to Mecca in 619 A.D.

After his return, the only shield he had against his enemies was Abu-Taleb, who soon died. A year later, in 620 A.D., his wife, financial supporter and benefactor, Khadijeh passed away at the age of 56. Upon the loss of his two supporters, he returned to preaching, contacting the people of Yasreb. In 622 A.D. he signed an agreement in Aqaba Mountain. Aqaba is near Mecca, Manna, and Jomreh, and it is the place where the Hajj pilgrims throw stones at the wall.

This agreement was the straw that broke the camel's back. Forty clan chiefs of the Ghoreysh tribe came together in Dar-ol-Naduh and decided to eliminate Mohammad. The time, place, and executor were chosen, and plans were laid out. Word got to Mohammad that he was to be killed in his bed at home, and so he decided that it was time to flee. He placed Ali in his stead in bed, and that night, together with Abu Bakr, Zayd father of Soudeh, and his new wife, fled from Mecca to Madina. This is referred to as hejrat, which means "migration." But it was not a voluntary migration; he ran away to save his life. That date was set as the starting point of the Islamic calendar. Some jokers say that had the people of Yasreb refused to meet with Mohammad, this entire episode might have been forgotten as an insignificant melancholic occurance, in a remote corner of the Arabian desert.

Mohammad, the Warrior and Commander

It was at this point that Mohammad made an about-face. His benevolent wife had died, her wealth spent. He had failed to amass a multitude of followers and supporters. His own clansmen were after his head. He was desperate. In Medina, with no means to support his handful of converts, he ordered them to begin robbing caravans. Thus, the very first band of Muslims became highway bandits. They joined the ranks of highwaymen of the caravan routes. He had to make a decision, and he did. He had learned that Arabs needed neither a preacher nor a guide. As a mass of people, they were hungry and scattered. Their basic occupation was warring and plundering. This way of life was so common and ordinary that the tribesmen had decided to declare three months of the year Haraam ("forbidden") months, during which to Arab raised a sword against another. That was prior to Mohammad's appearance. Mohammad changed that also.

He decided that he must unite the Arabs under one leadership, following one banner and ready to fight for the union. He decided that there was no one more worthy for the post of leadership than himself, and there was no better banner than the banner of Islam. He had to create a win-win situation for the desert wanderers to follow. It took time to come up with the right combination, but he did it.

In Medina he stayed at the house of Abu-Ayyub. Immediately after settling in the house he decided to build a mosque as a front against Kaaba, which later became his grave also. In the first year of his arrival in Medina he met with Salman the Farsi and others. This meeting and its subsequent cooperation between the two is an important event in the development of Islam, and will be presented in a separate book. The people of Medina were not amused with the mosque. They sought to avenge the Meccans in general and the tribe of Ghoreysh in particular. Mohammad was in a bind. He had to make a choice, and the only way out was a war. Thus Mohammad committed himself to his first war, known as Ghazaveh of Badr. We should note that Mohammad, in his 23-year reign as prophet-king of Arabia, instigated 83 wars. They were known as Ghazavat and Saraya. Ghazavats were wars in which Mohammad was personally involved, and Sarayas were those conducted by his commanders.

The War of Badr was fought on Friday, the 17th of the month of Ramazan, the second year of Hijrat (634 A.D.), in a place called Badr. The army of Mecca had 600 fighters, and Mohammad's army had 300. The commander of the Mecca forces was Abu-Jahl. In this war several well-known Ghoreysh leaders – namely Otba, Shabir, Valid ben-Otba, and Mina ben-Khalaf – were killed. This victory brought badly needed prestige to Mohammad. At the end of the war two prisoners of war were brought to Mohammad, Orba ben-Abi Moit and Nafar ben-Haresss. Mohamman knew them both well. Seeing them reminded him of their opposition to him, when they had declared, "We have seen your Koran; if you want, we can create a similar Koran." He ordered them beheaded. The person who had captured Nafar was Maghdad. He protested that Nafar was his prisoner and therefore his property. Mohammad replied, saying, "Have you forgotten his

opposition to the Koran?" Thus Mohammad, who would
brook no opposition, had Nafar killed. When it was Otba's
turn, Mohammad ordered Asem ben-Sabet to sever his
head. Othba screamed, "What is going to happen to my
children?" Mohammad replied, "All of you go to hell."

At that time in Medina there was a blind poetess by
the name of Asma, daughter of Marvan, from the Uss tribe.
In her poems she declared that Mohammad was the
stranger who chastised the people of Medina for their
sheep-like behavior toward him. She complained that a
person who had betrayed his own kinfolk and had killed
their commander in war was hardly justified in
proclaiming himself the Messenger of Allah, the
benevolent, the merciful. Mohammad called upon Amr
ben-Adi, Asma's divorced husband, and ordered him to kill
her. Amr dutifully entered Asma's house while she and her
children were asleep and while her youngest was nursing
at her breast. When Amr tried to remove the infant, Asma
awoke. He pushed the infant aside, grabbed Asma's throat
with one hand, and with the other stabbed her in the heart.
The following morning at prayer time, Mohammad was
informed about the killing. He asked Amr, "Have you
killed Marvan's daughter?" Amr replied "Yes."
Mohammad then turned to the people in the mosque and
said, "If you would like to know who has served Allah and
his Messenger, look at Amr."

Immediately after this bloody affair, Mohammad
committed his second crime. A 100-year-old poet by the
name of Abu-Akf was an opponent of Mohammad and his
new religion. In the midst of a group of followers,

Mohammad declared, "Which one of you will volunteer to release me from the harm of this man?" A recent convert, a member of the Bani-Omar, accepted the offer and killed Abu-Akf. For this, Mohammad praised him.

Mohammad needed more money and many more followers. In Mecca he had used Gabriel time and again to persuade people to believe and follow him. He now started using Gabriel again, but this time instead of preaching benevolence and mercy, he preached war and carnage. Mohammad saw that the Arabs had nothing to offer him, but in Medina there lived Jews of the Bani-Ghariza tribe who had an enviable social life and who had amassed great wealth. He approached them, proposing that they convert to Islam. They refused. Mohammad now needed an excuse to carry out his plan. He soon found one.

In front of a goldsmith's shop in the Jewish marketplace, a young Muslim girl was sitting, awaiting her order. An impish young Jewish boy managed to pin her skirt to the top of her dress so that when she tried to stand she found her skirt raised. She screamed and a Muslim man, who had witnessed the event, grabbed the Jewish boy by the neck and killed him. The Jews in the market attacked and killed the Muslim man in revenge. Word of this reached Mohammad, who had been hoping for such an occasion. He summoned his troops and surrounded the Jewish settlement. The Jews expected help from the Khazraj and would not surrender. After fifteen days of siege they realized that no help was forthcoming, and so they surrendered. The booty taken by Mohammad was substantial, and the remainder made his friends rich. His treatment of the Jews of Bani-Gharizeh created a new rift between Muslims and those who had refused to convert.

After the Bani-Gharizeh fiasco, another problem left a red spot on Mohammad's record. This was the execution of Kaab ebn-al-Ashraf. His crime, like that of Asma and Abu-Akf, was his poetry. Mohammad ordered Mohammad ben-Mosleme to kill Kaab. With the help of a gang's underhanded treachery, the task was accomplished. The gang attacked Kaab and cut him to pieces. They hurried to the mosque where Mohammad was awaiting the news. He congratulated them for their service and victory. When the gang members tossed Kaab's severed head at Mohammad's feet, he gleefully kicked it and praised Allah.

Mohammad's victory in the war of Badr led him into the war of Ohod. On the seventh day of Shavval, the third year after Hejrat, Abu-Sofyan, Akrame (son of Abu-Jahl, who had been killed by Mohammad in the previous year in the war of Badr), together with Safwan ben-Omayye, Khaled ben-Valid, and abu-Amr Raheb, marched toward Medina to avenge the death of those killed in Badr. They met Mohammad's army at the foothills of Ohod Mountain. Hamze, Mohammad's uncle, was killed and Mohammad was wounded, his head and face were bloodied. But by running from the battlefield he and his comrades survived. He lost some prestige, but his followers explained it away, saying that Allah wanted to examine their resolve. After the defeat, Mohammad decided that he should engage only in those battles where he was sure to be victorious.

In the fourth year of Hijrat, Abu-Bara, the head of the Bani-Amr clan, came to Medina. The Bani-Amr and Bani-Salim were two clans of the Havazan tribe who lived in the Najd area. Abu-Bara brought gifts for Mohammad, among them two horses and two camels. Mohammad agreed to accept the gifts on condition that Abu-Bara convert to Islam. Abu-Bara refused, saying that such a decision needed approval by the entire clan. He invited several of Mohammad's men to the clan for discussions. Mohammad accepted the offer and sent 40 of his followers to the Bani-Amr clan with a letter. They reached Birmuye in three days and sent a messenger to Amr ebn-al-Tofeil, the head of the Bani-Salim tribe, to deliver Mohammad's letter. Tofeil, without opening Mohammad's letter, ordered the messenger beheaded and issued an edict that not a single one of remaining 39 stay alive. The people of the Bani-Salim attacked the party of thirty-nine men and cut them to pieces – except for Amr ebn-Omayye, whowas away at the time and survived the massacre. The same fate befell six other messengers of Mohammad who had gone to deliver similar messages to al-Raji.

News of the massacre inflamed Mohammad. Every single day he prayed Allah to condemn those responsible. One month later, Mohammad told his followers that Gabriel had visited him with a message. The martyrs of Birmuye had asked Gabriel to tell Mohammad and his friends that they had met with Allah, who was very pleased. Mohammad ordered this message to be included in the Koran. It is interesting to note that later he changed his mine and ordered it removed. His daily curses and damnations had prepared his soldiers for an assault on

Bani-Salim.

On his way back to Medina, Amr ebn-Omayye, who
had survived the massacre, met with two members of Bani-
Amr clan.   In revenge he killed them while they were
asleep.   He later discovered that his two victims had
actually been messengers who had conferred with
Mohammad.   Mohammad admonished the killer, saying
that a restitution was called for.   To accomplish this,
Mohammad approached the Jews of the Bani-al-Nazir tribe,
who resided near the Bani-Amr tribe and were friendly
with them.   These Jews had signed treaties with Bani-Amr
and were well off financially.

The Bani-al-Nazir chiefs accepted Mohammad's
proposal, and Mohammad went to meet with them
accompanied by Abu Bakr and Osman.   In the middle of
the feast Mohammad vanished.   His two companions
searched for him everywhere, and when Omar and Osman
returned to the mosque, they found Mohammad there.
They asked what had happened.   Mohammad explained
that he had left for natural needs when Gabriel appeared to
him, warning that his life was in danger – "the Jews have
conspired against you."   Mohammad claimed to heed the
warning and so left.   It is noteworthy that the day after his
return he sent a message with Mohammad ben-Mosleme,
the murderer of Kaab ben-al-Ashraf, to the heads of Bani-
al-Nazir tribe, telling them that they had ten days to depart
from Medina, and if they refused they would all be killed.

The bewildered chiefs of Bani-al-Nazir told the
messenger that they had agreements and treaties with

Mohammad to live in peace. What kind of decision and demand is this, they demanded to know. Predicting this, Mohammad had coached Mohammad ben-Mosleme to respond: "Things have now changed. All agreements and treaties are nullified as of last night. As per the order issued by the Messenger of Allah, you have to leave Medina." When the Jews refused to leave, Mohammad was unable to disguise his ecstasy, screaming, "Allah is great, Allah is great, so the Jews have decided to fight!" He immediately summoned his warriors and armed them, and with Ali carrying the black banner, they started their march, surrounding and besieging the citadel.

The Bani-Gharizeh tribe, enemies of both Mohammad and Bani-al-Nazirm, stayed out of the battle. The following year Mohammad butchered them as well. Jews of Bani-al-Nazir fought courageously. In order to break their spirit, Mohammad did what no Arab had ever done in a tribal conflict: he ordered his soldiers to burn the date-palm trees. Moses had earlier condemned such act, declaring it inhuman. In response to the Jewish protest, Mohammad added a new verse to Chapter 59 of the Koran, Verse 5:

مَاقَطَعْتُمْ مِّنْ لِّينَةٍ ۞

أَوْتَرَكْتُمُوهَا قَآئِمَةً

عَلَىٰٓ أُصُولِهَا فَبِإِذْنِ ٱللَّهِ

وَلِيُخْزِىَ ٱلْفَـٰسِقِينَ

"Whether ye cut down the tender palm trees, or ye left them standing on their roots, it was by leave of Allah,

and in order that He might cover with shame the rebellious transgressions."

After three weeks of siege Jews finally accepted Mohammad's terms, but now Mohammad upped his requirements saying that they may depart but had to leave all their belongings behind for his soldiers. Thus did the doomed Jews of Bani-al-Nazir begin their long march toward Syria, Khaibar and Jericho. On the grounds that his soliers had not used their swords, Mohammad took possession of all the fertile Jewish lands, without sharing any valuable item with anyone. He then followed Verse 5 with a newly inspired Verse 6:

(٦) وَمَآ أَفَآءَ ٱللَّهُ عَلَىٰ رَسُولِهِۦ مِنۡهُمۡ

فَمَآ أَوۡجَفۡتُمۡ عَلَيۡهِ مِنۡ خَيۡلٍ وَلَا رِكَابٍ

وَلَٰكِنَّ ٱللَّهَ يُسَلِّطُ رُسُلَهُۥ عَلَىٰ مَن يَشَآءُ

وَٱللَّهُ عَلَىٰ كُلِّ شَيۡءٍ قَدِيرٌ

"What Allah has bestowed on His Messenger (and taken away) from them – for this ye made no expedition with their cavalry or camelry: but Allah gives power to His Messenger over any He pleases: and Allah has power over all things."

The expulsion of Bani-al-Nazir and the seizure of their belongings strengthened Mohammad's economic as well as financial situation tremendously.

A few months later, Mohammad was informed that some clans of the north-west area, near the Red Sea, were conspiring against him.   He ordered his army to assemble, and in a rapid march he reached the wells of al-Murisi in eight days. He established his camp near Mecca.

Mohammad normally took two of his wives with him on military expeditions. He chose them by drawing names. So on this trip Aysha and Ome Salameh were with him.   By the time people of Bani-al-Mostalaq became aware of Mohammad's presence in was too late. A shower of arrows fell on them, they were captured, and they all became prisoners of Mohammad's army. Mohammad enslaved two-hundred Jewish families and seized two thousand camels, five thousand sheep and goats, and many household goods. He took twenty percent of all the loot and gave the rest, including the enslaved women and girls, to his soldiers for their carnal use. Some of the Bani-al-Mostaalaq men, unable to withstand the barbaric aggressions upon their women folk, resisted. Mohammad ordered that they all be beheaded and that the copulations take place beside their beheaded corpses.

Among the enslaved women on the tribe there was a most beautiful girl called Joviriye, daughter of Haress ben-abi-Dira, who became part of Mohammad's harem, and in the next few days played a significant role in Mohammad's life.   The plunder and pillage of Bani-al-Mostaalaq enriched Mohammad's treasury by leaps and bounds.

On the return home, Ayshe wandered away from the camp for personal reasons and was left behind. A rider, one of the most handsome in the army, found her and put her on his camel, reaching Medina two days later. This mishap created a major problem for Mohammad and his right-hand man Ali. There was no choice but to ask for Allah's intervention to set things straight. Allah, with the help of Gabriel, immediately inspired 22 Verses of Chapter 24, which Mohammad added to the Koran, forgiving all and excusing everyone.

Rumors of this episode had not completed their rounds in Muslim circles and so had not yet been forgotten, when one day Mohammad entered the house of his adopted son Zayd ebn-Haress. Zayd was not home and his wife, Zeynab, daughter of Jahesh, was bathing, unaware of Mohammad's presence. She was startled when she saw him at the doorway and tried to cover herself, but Mohammad had already seen what he should not have seen. Through the archangel's aid several more Verses were added to help Mohammad ask his adopted son to divorce his wife so that he could have her instead. Allah obliged and furnished Gabriel and Mohammad with Verses 4, 37, and 40 of Chapter 33, Making all this legal.

Verse 4:

مَّا جَعَلَ ٱللَّهُ لِرَجُلٍ مِّن قَلْبَيْنِ فِى جَوْفِهِۦ وَمَا جَعَلَ أَزْوَٰجَكُمُ ٱلَّٰٓـِٔى تُظَٰهِرُونَ مِنْهُنَّ أُمَّهَٰتِكُمْ وَمَا جَعَلَ أَدْعِيَآءَكُمْ أَبْنَآءَكُمْ ذَٰلِكُمْ قَوْلُكُم بِأَفْوَٰهِكُمْ وَٱللَّهُ يَقُولُ ٱلْحَقَّ وَهُوَ يَهْدِى ٱلسَّبِيلَ

"Allah has not made for any man two hearts in his (one) body: nor has He made your wives whom ye divorce by Zihar your mothers: nor has He made your adopted sons your sons. Such is (only) your (manner of) speech by your mouths. But Allah tells (you) the truth, and He shows the (right) way."

Verse 37:

وَإِذْ تَقُولُ لِلَّذِى ﴿٣٧﴾

أَنْعَمَ اللَّهُ عَلَيْهِ وَأَنْعَمْتَ عَلَيْهِ

أَمْسِكْ عَلَيْكَ زَوْجَكَ وَاتَّقِ اللَّهَ

وَتُخْفِى فِى نَفْسِكَ مَا اللَّهُ

مُبْدِيهِ وَتَخْشَى النَّاسَ وَاللَّهُ

أَحَقُّ أَن تَخْشَاهُ

فَلَمَّا قَضَى زَيْدٌ مِّنْهَا وَطَرًا

زَوَّجْنَاكَهَا لِكَىْ لَا يَكُونَ

عَلَى الْمُؤْمِنِينَ حَرَجٌ

فِى أَزْوَاجِ أَدْعِيَآئِهِمْ

إِذَا قَضَوْا مِنْهُنَّ وَطَرًا

وَكَانَ أَمْرُ اللَّهِ مَفْعُولًا

"Behold! Thou didst say to one who had received the grace of Allah and thy favour: 'Retain thou (in wedlock) thy wife, and fear Allah.' But thou didst hide in thy heart that which Allah was about to make manifest: thou didst fear the people, but it is more fitting that you shouldst fear

Allah. Then when Zayd had dissolved (his marriage) with her, with the necessary (Formality), we joined her in marriage to thee: in order that (in future) there may be no difficulty to the believers in (the matter of) marriage with the wives of their adopted sons, when the latter have dissolved with the necessary (formality) (their marrage) with them. And Allah's command must be fulfilled."

Verse 40:

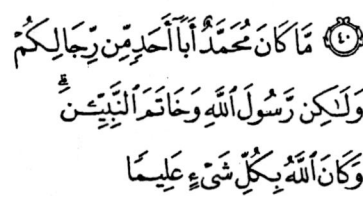

"Mohammad is not the father of any of your men, but (he is) the Messenger of Allah, and the seal of Prophets: and Allah has full knowledge of all things."

In the month of Zel-Ghaad in the fifth year of Hijrat, the people of Ghoreysh were planning to avenge their previous losses, as well as the losses of their Jewish friends.   They amassed an army of 10,000 against Mohammad and his allies. This news reached Mohammad, and he was frightened, for he remembered his defeat in the War of Ohod, where the army of Mecca was only 3,000. Now with 10,000 in the army, he called an emergency council. Among the councilors was a man by the name of Rouzbeh Mehyar (an Iranian name) nicknamed Salman Farsi, who was born in a Zoroastrian household in the village of Jee near Isfahan.   In his youth, due to the depressed economy of Sassanid era, he left for Syria and became a Christian. He was enslaved in a Macedonian war and was purchased by a Jewish man from the Bani-Kalb tribe. Later, he became a Muslim and was purchased and freed from bondage. With his experience of modern warfare, he advised Mohammad that the only way to face the Ghoreysh army was to dig a moat around the city of Medina. The moat was dug in six days. Houses outside of the moat were vacated and their residents moved into the city. Thus a Muslim army of 3,000 was able and ready to face the 10,000-strong army of the Ghoreysh. This battle came to be known as the War of the Moat.

The Ghoreyshi army was surprised upon reaching the moat. Abu Sofyan, their commander, thought it best to make a deal with the Jews of the Bani-Gharizeh. A messenger by the name of Siaa met with Kaab ebn-Asad, chief of the Bani-Gharizeh, who agreed to join the battle. But when the time came to act, the Bani-Gharizeh did not. Meanwhile the battle started and Mohammad was worried. The step-by-step recall of this battle can be read in many books. The interesting point is that Ali used trickery to beat Amr, and Mohammad made sure to praise Ali's trickery, declaring that war is basically nothing but deceit and trickery. In this respect, it is noteworthy that Chapter 7, Verse 183; Chapter 68, Verse 45; Chapter 8, Verse 30; Chapter 3, Verse 54; and Chapter 4, Verse 142 all indicate not only that Ali and Mohammad are tricky, but that Allah Himself is the trickiest of them all.

Now that Mohammad had the Bani-Gharizeh involved, he decided that he should complete the work the way he thought it should be done. He dispatched Naim ebn-Masud and two others to meet with the chiefs of Bani-Gharizeh and say, "Now that you are siding with the Ghoreysh, it will be wise if you take several hostages from the Ghoreysh, just in case they decide to leave you by yourselves to face Mohammad." The Bani-Gharizeh leaders thought this a good idea and agreed. Naim, after finishing this dirty work with the Jews, met with the leaders of Ghoreysh, telling them, "I understand that the Bani-Gharizeh regret having sided with you, and have sent people to meet with Mohammad and express their regret. Because they do not trust you, they have asked for hostages. In reality they want those hostages to prove to Mohammad that their regret is sincere. They will surrender them to Mohammad as proof of their claim." The trick worked, and the next morning a messenger was dispatched to the Bani-Gharizeh telling them to attack the following day. The Bani-Gharizeh were bewildered, saying that since the following day was the Sabbath, they could not attack. Thus the treaty was nullified, and the two did not join forces against Mohammad. Ghoreysh had an additional problem – not enough feed for their horses. Many of their animals died of hunger. Unfortunately for the Ghoreishi army, the day of the battle was stormy. All the negative factors combined to demoralize the army, and Abu Sofyan decided to retreat. He got on a camel and rode toward Mecca, and Khaled with 200 riders followed the army to defend the rear against possible attack from Mohammad.

Mohammad, relieved from a tight spot, called his commanders, saying that Gabriel had informed him that Allah had sent the sandstorm to help the Muslims, and that Gabriel further told him that since the Ghoreysh had decided not to fight, it was the best time for them to finish the Jews. Soldiers, beleaguered from fifteen days of siege, protested. Mohammad screamed at them, saying, "Did the Angels of Allah put down their arms that you are trying to put down yours? They poured sand and stones on the enemy to destroy them. Gabriel told me get up and go after the Jews and cut them to pieces."

Balal (he was one of Mohammad's followers who called for prayer – Azan) received his orders from Mohammad and went into town on Medina inviting people to join Mohammad's army for the march against the Jews. Mohammad's 3,000-strong army surrounded the citadel and besieged it for 15 days. The Bani-Gharizeh surrendered, but Mohammad would not accept. He left it to the judgment of the elders of Uss tribe who were friendly with the Bani-Gharizeh. That did it. First the men and young boys of the Bani-Gharizeh were brought out of their homes with their hands tied behind their backs. Then the women and young girls were marched in front of Mohammad. Mohammad took the most beautiful one, Reyhaneh, and sent her to his harem. The rest of the women were divided among the soldiers and Mohammad. Then it was time to divide the rest of the loot, including household goods, arms, and animals. The tragedy of the Bani-Gharizeh was the second phase of Mohammad's plan for the Jews. The judgment of Uss was that Mohammad should let the Jews go, but Mohammad then left the final judgment to Saad ben-Moaz, who had been wounded in the battle and was after revenge. When he was brought in to state his decision, he asked Mohammad, "Do you promise and will carry out my judgment, with the help of Allah?"

All present indicated that they would. His declaration was such: "Kill all the men and young boys. The women and children are to be taken prisoners and to be sold as slaves. All their belongings are to be confiscated and divided among the soldiers – minus 20 percent, which goes to Mohammad." Mohammad, with a smile in his face, raised his hands and declared that he would obey Allah's wishes.

The morning after passing the judgment, per Mohammad's order, a great ditch was dug. All the men and young boys were brought to the edge of the ditch in groups of five and six, where they were beheaded. It took the entire day to behead 800 men and boys. That night was a festive carnal orgy with the enslaved womenfolk of the Bani-Gharizeh. Words cannot describe the anguish and pain of Reyhaneh, who had to sleep with Mohammad, the man who had killed her father, husband, brother, and all the men of her tribe. The next day, Mohammad, in order to legitimize his copulation, asked her to marry him. She replied that she would rather remain a slave but would never make this carnal relationship legitimate. The poor woman died at the age of 20 in the year of 627 A.D. Things were not all right yet, for the ferocity of the action had to be legitimized. Thus a group of Verses were added to Chapter 33, whereby Allah expressed His pleasure and satisfaction with Mohammad's action.

In the spring of the sixth year of Hijrat (628 A.D.) Mohammad decided to visit Kaaba. With 1,600 soldiers he started toward Mecca. He was met with some people from the Ghoreysh who convinced him not to go there. They signed an agreement stating that Mohammad can visit the

next year. Mohammad returned to Medina. Unwilling to
let a year go by without a venture, upon his return to
Medina he wrote letters to the courts of Iran, Yemen,
Egypt, and Abyssinia inviting them to accept Islam. There
were no takers.

He needed funds. About one hundred miles to the
north of Medina was a fertile area called Kheybar where
Jews lived. It has seven citadels, one inside the other, that
were called Katye, Naem, Shagh, Ghamus, Natch, Tabh,
and Salalem.   Ali, who had just married Mohammad's
daughter Fateme, was with him in this expedition.   The
Jews of Kheybar were caught by surprise, so much so that
their allies, the tribe of Bani-Ghaffan, could not come to
their help.

Mohammad began his attacks from the surrounding
villages.   Upon conquering each village, he ordered the
water-wells filled with stones and dirt and their palm trees
set afire. Then one citadel after the other fell to the Islamic
army. The Jews offered to surrender all their belongings
and go. When Kananeh ben-Rabi and his nephew tried to
leave, Mohammad called him and said, "I know you have
jewels that are not part of this loot, where are they?"
Kananeh replied, "We are at your mercy. If you find
anything, do with us as you please." Kananeh's cousin
knew the hiding place and told Mohammad where to find
them.   Mohammad dispatched several followers, who
returned with a chest filled with jewels. Mohammad asked
for the rest of the jewels and was told that there were none.
He ordered his troops to lay Kananeh and his nephew on
their backs on the floor and to disrobe their chests and

cover their chests with burning wood. The human fireplace burned and the victims screamed while their flesh was being broiled. All of this was done in the presence of Kananeh's wife, Saffiyeh, who had the misfortune of having to copulate with Mohammad that night and become part of his harem.

Mohammad, jubilant at this victory, ordered a feast for that night. Among the cooks was a woman named Zeynab, sister of Marhab. She had a lamb killed, cooked it for Mohammad and his friends, and had it poisoned. Mohammad took the shoulder, his favorite part, and left the rest for Abu Bakr and the others. Mohammad tasted something wrong with his first bite, which happened to be where the poison was concentrated. He stopped eating and ordered all others to stop also. One of his friends, who had already swallowed some, had turned dark and died. Although Mohammad spat the food out, he injected enough poison to give him an extreme stomach pain. He summoned Zeynab and inquired why she had tried to poison him. She replied, "You have killed my father, brother, uncle, husband, and the rest of my relatives, did you expect otherwise from me?" He ordered her beheaded on the spot.

With this last victory, Mohammad cleared Arabian Peninsula of the Jews. From that day no Jewish person has ever lived or worshipped in Arabia.

Upon his return from his military-sexual-criminal expedition, Mohammad took Ome-Jeyb, daughter of Abu-Sofyan, as his wife. He also married the 17-year-old wife of the broiled Kananeh as his tenth wife. He was 60 years old at the time.

In the month of Ramazan, the eighth year of Hejrat, Mohammad, at the age of 62, decided to conquer Mecca, the crown jewel of Arabia. With 10,000 soldiers he marched toward Mecca, and in a place called Khandame the two armies met. Negotiated victory was with Mohammad, and on the 12th day of January 630 Mohammad entered the city.

When the Muslim forces conquered Mecca, they took possession of Kaaba and destroyed 360 idols that belonged to 360 Arab tribes.

Some of Mohammad's followers were from Medina, and they asked that the entire population of Mecca be annihilated. Mohammad, however, declared a general amnesty for all with the exception of the following people: Safvan ben-Omayye, Abdollah ben-Khata, Moghis ben-Sabab, Akrameh son of Abu-Jahl, Haress ben-Naghiz ben-Wahab, and Abdolah ben-Saad ben-Abisareh. The last-named had long been Mohammad's steno-secretary, and at times used to play dirty tricks with the dictated verses. This secretary had abandoned Islam on the grounds that "if what Mohammad dictates comes from Allah, then how is it that my actions change them and that he agrees with them?" That bought him his death sentence.

Other than the people on Mohammad's black list, two poets known as Fartaneh and Gharibeh, who had poked fun at Mohammad, and two women known as Hend Bent

Atba and Sara Mula Amr ben-Hashem, who had ridiculed
him when he lived in Mecca, were also executed.

Mohammad became the sole ruler of Arabia with
the exception of Hanin, with its two tribes, Hozan and
Saghif. Mohammad wanted Hanin included in his empire,
and so with 10,000 soldiers he began his march. Islamic
forces were now addicted to plunder, and instead of
fighting at the initial stages of the battle, they began to loot.
The battle was being lost when Mohammad, Ali, and Abu-
Sofian, by screaming and barking orders called them to
order. Most of the opposition fled to Taef with Mohammad
in hot pursuit. The Muslims surrounded Taef and kept it
under siege for 17 days. The Muslim losses were
substantial, and Mohammad ordered retreat without a
victory.

In the tenth year of Hijrat, Mohammad went on Hajj
to Mecca. This was his last visit there. Upon his return
from Hajj, he tried to send a military expedition to Syria
but took ill. His sickness grew worse, and finally on the
ninth day of June 623, at the age of 63, he passed away.
The world has seldom, if ever, seen a man like him. He
was a master strategist, a brave fighter, a vicious adversary,
a superb tactician, a brilliant planner, a fantastic love-
maker, a cool butcher, a merciless avenger, a fearful hater,
with many other attributes, good and bad, that seldom come
together in one man.

With the knowledge that what he preached was
copied from other religions, Mohammad accomplished his
goal to unite the Arabs, establish a kingdom, become rich

beyond all his imaginings, and be the king pf Arabia. He did all that and died as the supreme ruler of his established kingdom. He still rules that vast Muslim Empire. The Muslim Empire governs over one point two (1.2) billion people. Every single day, every single Muslim in the world prostrates in prayer toward Mecca five times a day and recites the chant, "There is no God but Allah, Mohammad is the Messenger of Allah." This life-long practice will brainwash anyone. Every Muslim (who can afford to) goes to Hajj at least once in his or her life, pays twenty percent taxes on his income or plunder, and fasts for one month of the lunar year. These practices make one a good Muslim, guaranteeing entrance to the Islamic Paradise.

According to Muslim teachings, this world has nothing to offer. One is born to work for Islam and go to Paradise. In Islam, one can go to Paradise in one of three ways: (1) one can be a good Muslim all his life; (2) one can convert an infidel, or kill an infidel; or (3) one can participate in Jihad. The awards for being a good Muslim are many, and penalties for not being one are much more. It is permissible to keep one's religion, provided one follows the Torah, the Gospel, or the Avesta, but one has to pay taxes called Jazyeh. If a person's religion does not come from one of these volumes, then he is an infidel and must be killed. A Muslim man can have four wives at any given time, and divorce and marry as many times as he pleases, so long as the total number of wives at any given time is not above four. A Muslim can have as many Sigheh (contract wives) as he pleases, even for the short duration of a one-time copulation (legitimized prostitution), and the clergy drafts the contract (acting as sort of a pimp). The term of stay in Islamic Paradise is forever. Whatever a Bedouin Arab would desire is there for him: a river of wine, a river of honey, and a river of milk are promised. Yet, that is not good enough for the Bedouin. He, upon his entry, will receive 72 ever-virgin girls known as Houries and his masculine virility will be increased a hundred-fold. His physical body will be restored to his prime body of thirty years of age. If he likes young beautiful boys, he may select as many Gholmans (pretty boys) as he pleases.

Islamic Hell is the destination of bad Muslims and the rest of the entire non-Muslim world. **Islamic Paradise and Hell** will be presented under a separate cover. Islam began with Mohammad, but it did not end with Mohammad. The Koran, by itself, does not define Islam either. There are also the Hadiss (traditions) and Sonnat (practices) that are as powerful, if not more so, than the Koran. These also will be examined separately. There are hundreds of books used and quoted by the Muslim clerics that govern the Muslim life and **modus operandi.** These will be examined separately.

And finally, what do we mean by "TWO FACES OF ISLAM"? Unlike any other religion, Islam can be benevolent and merciful, and in a split second can change into a ferocious doctrine. It all depends on who is implementing it and for what purpose. Part of the Koran was written while Mohammad was in Mecca and was a preacher. While in Mecca, he was poor and needed help; thus he preached benevolence. While he was married to Khadijeh and she provided for him, he did not need help for himself, but for others. But, after Khadijeh's death, there was no help coming for him and his followers. He and his followers had to resort to robbery – first attacking caravans. When Mohammad soon realized that being a common thief was beneath his dignity, he began to plunder others in the name of Allah and His Messenger. He had established that he was His only Messenger, and he could produce as many Verses that he pleased to justify his behavior.

To entice the Bedouin to follow him and plunder, he established the needed rule, which we can paraphrase as: "Come and fight for me and for Allah. If you get killed, I will vouch for you, and you will go to Paradise. If you win, because you have already fought for Islam, you are Paradise-bound anyway, but while here on Earth, you'll receive 80 percent of what you plunder and give 20 percent to Mohammad." This policy guaranteed absolute obedience. It was and is a win-win proposition. Since disobedience is going to take one to Hell, no one dares to disobey.

It was not only the loot that attracted converts. All the women and children that were taken into slavery were divided among the faithful. Women can be kept as Keniz, a slave for carnal use or a house servant. Slaves can be traded back to their families for 4,000 derhams (unit of money), or sold in the market as a slave. Most of the black American slaves bought by white traders and brought to the New World and sold to the plantation owners had been purchased from Muslim enslavers.

Since Islam is a combination of religion, law and government, a Muslim does not have to follow any other

government, law, or religion.   By disobeying other
authorities he is participating in Jihad and is therefore
Paradise-bound.   Since the ultimate goal of any Muslim is
to do what it takes to get to Paradise, why should one take
chances?

What is the Koran?

The Koran, in general, is referred to as (Kalam Ollah Majid) by the Iranians, which means "The Glorious Words of Allah." For the bielievers who do not read and understand Arabic it may be acceptable. But those who read Arabic and understand what they read may have some problems. For those who are literate in Arabic, and who have read other religions' holy books and who knows the history of religions, there are a lot of problems, and they usually reject the claims of the Koran - unless, of couse, their lives are at stake.

Mohammad had no choice but to invoke divine intervention. He also had no choice but to produce a book and call it the inspired words of Allah brought to him through Gabriel. Without these ploys he could never have done what he did and survived people's wrath. He needed the carrot and the stick. He needed the promised goodies of Paradise and the threat of everlasting tortures of the Islamic Hell. The Koran contains benevolence as well as eternal damnation in Hell and on Earth while alive. Verses of the Koran were recorded during Mohammad's lifetime but not put together as a book. It was Osman, the third Caliph, who gathered the scattered Verses and created the Koran that we know. There was no particular order for the Verses to be put together. There are contradictions, and there are Verses poorly copied from the Torah and the Gospels. All these Verses were assembled into a book to be used to control and encourage the Bedouins to follow commands. Without the Koran and the other books that followed, Mohammad's conquest would have stopped at the borders of the Arabian Peninsula.

It is said that at the time there were four books assembled as the Korans. That was unacceptable. It is said that three of them were destroyed and only one kept for the posterity. The Koran that we know is composed of 6,236 Verses in 114 Surehs (Chapters). Of these, 4,904 Verses are attributed to Mecca and 1,332 to Medina. Although he lived 10 years in Medina, and preached only a short time in Mecca, he was totally occupied with wars and massacres while in Medina.

There are 91 negative Verses in 28 Surehs. Eight of those Verses in five Surehs contain direct orders from Allah to kill. Two Verses in two Surehs introduce Jihad. Two Verse in two Surehs condemn women. Twenty-eight Verses in twenty-one Surehs promise perpetual-virgin women for men who go to Paradise.

For the satisfaction of those who claim that the Koran is all peace and benevolence, refer to Verse 5-9 of Chapter 93.

Verse 5:

ﮩ وَلَسَوْفَ يُعْطِيكَ رَبُّكَ فَتَرْضَىٰ

"And soon will thy Guardian-Lord give thee (that wherewith) thou shall be well-pleased."

Verse 6:

ﮪ أَلَمْ يَجِدْكَ يَتِيمًا فَآوَىٰ

" *Did he not find thee an orphan and give thee shelter (and care)?* "

Verse 7:

وَوَجَدَكَ ضَالًّا فَهَدَىٰ ۝

"*And He found thee wandering, and He gave thee guidance.*"

Verse 8:

وَوَجَدَكَ عَائِلًا فَأَغْنَىٰ ۝

"*And He found thee in need, and made thee independent.*"

Verse 9:

فَأَمَّا الْيَتِيمَ فَلَا تَقْهَرْ ۝

"*Therefore treat not the orphan with harshness.*"

For those who claim that there are no Verses in the Koran where Allah advocates killing, we reproduce the following Verses:

Chapter 2, Verse 191:

وَاقْتُلُوهُمْ حَيْثُ ثَقِفْتُمُوهُمْ وَأَخْرِجُوهُم مِّنْ حَيْثُ أَخْرَجُوكُمْ وَالْفِتْنَةُ أَشَدُّ مِنَ الْقَتْلِ وَلَا تُقَاتِلُوهُمْ عِندَ الْمَسْجِدِ الْحَرَامِ حَتَّىٰ يُقَاتِلُوكُمْ فِيهِ فَإِن قَاتَلُوكُمْ فَاقْتُلُوهُمْ كَذَٰلِكَ جَزَاءُ الْكَافِرِينَ ۝

*"And slay them wherever ye catch them, and turn
them out from where they have turned you out, for tumult
and oppression are worse than slaughter; ..."*

Chapter 9, Verse 29:

$$\text{﴿٢٩﴾ قَٰتِلُوا الَّذِينَ لَا يُؤْمِنُونَ بِاللَّهِ}$$
$$\text{وَلَا بِالْيَوْمِ الْآخِرِ وَلَا يُحَرِّمُونَ مَا حَرَّمَ اللَّهُ}$$
$$\text{وَرَسُولُهُ وَلَا يَدِينُونَ دِينَ الْحَقِّ}$$
$$\text{مِنَ الَّذِينَ أُوتُوا الْكِتَٰبَ}$$
$$\text{حَتَّىٰ يُعْطُوا الْجِزْيَةَ عَن يَدٍ وَهُمْ صَٰغِرُونَ}$$

*"Fight those who believe not in Allah nor the Last
Day, nor hold that forbidden which hath been forbidden by
Allah and His Messenger..."*

Chapter 33, Verse 61:

$$\text{﴿٦١﴾ مَلْعُونِينَ أَيْنَمَا ثُقِفُوا أُخِذُوا وَقُتِّلُوا تَقْتِيلًا}$$

*"They shall have a curse on them: wherever they
are found, they shall be seized and slain."*

Chapter 47, Verse 4: $\text{﴿٤﴾ فَإِذَا لَقِيتُمُ الَّذِينَ كَفَرُوا فَضَرْبَ الرِّقَابِ حَتَّىٰ}$

$$\text{إِذَا أَثْخَنتُمُوهُمْ فَشُدُّوا الْوَثَاقَ فَإِمَّا مَنًّا بَعْدُ وَإِمَّا فِدَاءً حَتَّىٰ تَضَعَ الْحَرْبُ أَوْزَارَهَا ذَٰلِكَ وَلَوْ يَشَاءُ اللَّهُ}$$
$$\text{لَانتَصَرَ مِنْهُمْ وَلَٰكِن لِّيَبْلُوَا بَعْضَكُم بِبَعْضٍ وَالَّذِينَ قُتِلُوا فِي سَبِيلِ اللَّهِ فَلَن يُضِلَّ أَعْمَالَهُمْ}$$

"Therefore, when ye meet the unbelievers (in fight) smite at their necks...."

The sad conclusion is that a Muslim has no mind of his own and is an implement in the hands of his Mojtahed (religious leader, teacher). Unfortunately Mujtaheds are not their own men either, and they are controlled and directed by others. The Koran says, (Do not say "I will do it tomorrow.' You should say "Allah willing I will do it tomorrow,' because nothing happens without His will. Not even a leaf falls from the tree without His will."

Unfortunately there is no Homeland in Islam for many Muslim Nations. The Qiblah is Mecca, and the Home is Kaaba.

With this booklet, in this format, we are trying to provide this great nation of ours truthful and valid information about Islam. A single book such as this cannot and will not cover the entire subject. We see it as our mission to provide and distribute the necessary books that can illuminate the minds of American public concerning Islam and Muslims in their relations with each other.

Bibliography

Abdullah Yusuf Ali, *The Meaning of The Holy Quran.*
Amana Publications, Beltsville, Maryland, U.S.A.
(Arabic/English)

Hasan Abbasi, *From Mitra to Mohammad.* Homa
Publications, Parsi (Farsi)

Ali Mir-Fetros, *Islamology.* Afra Publications, Paris,
France. Parsi (Farsi)

Alkashaf al-Haqiqah al-Tanzil, al-Zamakhshari. Cairo.
(Arabic)

Al-Ghazi, Mohamad ebn-Omar al-Vakid. (Arabic)

Grishman, *Iran from Beginning Till Islam.* Translated by
Dr. Moin, Nashre Ketab Publications. Los Angeles.
(Farsi)

Dr. Roshangar, *Koran Re-Studied.* Pars Publications. San
Fransisco. (Farsi)

Ali Dashti, *Twenty Three Years. (Farsi)*

Gen, Sir Persi Six, *History of Iran.* Translated by
Mohammad Taghi, Fakhr-Daii. (Farsi)

Abdol-Hosein Zarrin-Kub, *History on Balance.* Amir
Kabir Publications. (Farsi)

Abdol-Azim Rezaii, *Ten Thousand Years History of Iran.*
Eqbal Publications. (Farsi)

Mohammad ben-Jarir Tabari. *Tarikh Tabari.* (Farsi)

Hosein Pirnia, *Unabridged History of Iran.* Ebn Sina
Publications. (Farsi)

Jalal-ed-din Abdol-Rahman Syuti. *Tafsir Jalalin.* Cairo
(Arabic)

Gustav Lobone. *Arab and Islamic Civilization.* Translated
by Mohammed Taghi Daii. (Farsi)

Mohammad Bagher Majlesi. *Hita al-Mottaghin.* Taheri
Publications. (Farsi)

Mohammad Bagher Majlesi. *Hayat ol-qlub* or *Life of
Mohammad.* (Farsi)

Abdol-Hosein Zarkub. *Two Centuries of Silence.* Navid
Publications. (Farsi)

Abdol-Molk ebn-Hashem. *Life of Mohammad.* (Farsi)

Ebn-Eshaq. *Sirat ol-Rasul.* (Farsi)

Dr Roshangar. *Shiism and Mahdism.* Pars Publications,
San Francisco. (Farsi)

Mohammed ben-Esmail al-Bokhari. *Sahih al-Bokhari.*
Cairo. (Arabic)

Ebn-Saad. *Tabaqar al-Kabir.* (Arabic)

M.A. Fajr. *Fajr Islam.* Amir Kabir Publications. (Farsi)

Elahi Qamshi. *Koran Karim.* Islamic Publications
Foundation. (Farsi)

Holy Bible. *Old and New Testament.* International Bible
Society. (Farsi)

Dr. Roshangar. *Cyrus the Great and Mohammed ben-
Abdullah.* Pars Publications, San Francisco. (Farsi)

Allame Vaez Shafti (pseudonym). *Koran Kalame
Mohammad.* New Horizon Publication. (Farsi)

Bijan Fakhur (pseudonym). *Mohammad, Prophet King of
Arabia.* New Horizon Publication. (Farsi)

Anwar Sheikh. *Islam, the Arab Nationalist Movement.* The
Principality Publication, London. (English)

Ibn Hasham. *Sira Rasul Allah.* Ed. F. Wustenfield, 1959-
60.

G. Sachau. *Mohammed and Mohammedanism.* London
Rivitons. (English)

Martin Ling. *Mohammed: His Life Based on the Earliest Sources.* London, 1983. (English)

D.S. Marfoliouth. *Mohammed and the Rise of Islam.* London, 1905. (English)

William Muir. *The Life of Mohammed.* Edinburgh: John Grant, 1923. (English)

A. Spencer, ed. *Al-Wakiki, Al-Moghazi.* Calcutta, 1856.

The book you just finished reading was a verbal portrait of the functional life of Mohammad, son of Ameneh and Abdullah, creator and promoter of Islam. He died at the age of 63 without choosing a successor or establishing a government. Islam, a way of life that he invited people to accept, is an Arabic word and means total submission or surrender. He invented Islam to be implemented by him to make him rich and powerful. Islam as a religion as well as a government, law, and economic ideology was established after his death.

BOOK 2

Formation of the Empire

ADDENDUM

Originally, Book 2 was published in a separate cover, however, due to requests of many readers, it was logical to publish them in one volume. It is believed that Islam would not have been initiated had it not been for Mohammad, and it would not have survived had it not been for the functions of the first four Khalifehs.

Mohammad united Arabia by implementing Islam, and the first four Khalifehs developed it into an aggressive, looting, plundering, and expanding government. Islam changed and evolved. It branched out and took different shapes and forms, but it never lost its original premise, that is the **subjugation of the entire world.** All that has already taken place can not and should not be covered in one book. Islam has become belligerent again, and we are now witnessing further changes and aggressions on the part of Islam.

With this series of books we intend to inform the non-Muslim world that Islam is not just another religion. Mohammad began this movement and stated that the "World is divided in two camps, the world of Islam and the world of war. This war shall continue until the entire world becomes Muslim."

Book 2 provides you with an overview of what took place after Mohammad's death. History books and other books that have recently been written and published will provide you with further information. We are indeed fortunate that we are living in an era that people are not terrified any more and do write the truth.

In this book we have departed from the customary practice and have included pages that are not numbered. Had we not done that, the two books would have merged together and lost part of the intent. Please forgive and forgo this intrusion. The next page is page 48.

Introduction

In book 1 of the **Two Faces of Islam** we briefly covered the life of Mohammad, emphasizing the most influential events in the formation of his character. In this book we intend to inform you, the reader, how and why he made   certain decisions and their aftermath that later became the law for his followers and immediate successors, as well as the rest of the Islamic world that followed.

Abu al-Qasem Mohammad ebn-Abdollah ebn-abd-ol Motalleb ebn-al-Hashem, the inventor and founder of Islam and of the premise of Arab/Islam Empire that was created after his death, was in Mecca about 570 A.D. Mohammed, as mentioned in Book 1, belonged to the clan of Hashem, one of the clans of the tribe of Ghoreysh. The Ghoreysh were descendents of Esmail (Ishmael), son of Abraham, the Jewish patriarch. Arabs claim that it was Abraham, accompanied by Esmail, who built the temple of Kaaba for the worship of God, which for centuries had been the center of Arab idolatry.

Mohammad tried to free himself from hunger and poverty and ended up being the prophet-king of a united Arabia. Others came later, adopted his procedure, altered it, formed it into documents and created a doctrine, and produced a long lasting empire called Islam.

Since Mohammad had no role models, he learned the hard way. He improvised on demand to fit the situation. There were two neighboring empires, namely the Persian and Byzantine empires, but he had no access to either administrative and military structures, procedures, and bylaws.

The common denominators among the various Arabian tribes were: the Arabic language, pagan Arab rituals and rights, poverty, lack of food, lack of social life, nine months of war and plunder in each year among themselves, non-existence of ethics, and various other unpleasant and harmful factors . Mohammad, being a bright and ambitious person, had observed and studied all of these factors during his miserable and poverty-stricken childhood and youth.

To free himself from poverty and hunger Mohammad needed wealth and power, which meaning possessions and followers. Although he had patterned his religion after the three other religions, he soon found out that it would not do. He learned that the Bedouins would follow him only and only if he could offer them a win-win situation. Yet even that by itself would not do either. He also needed a device for admonishment and foreboding. He created the imaginary Islamic Hell for the afterlife together with the real hell that he imposed on those who disobeyed his law and command.

The entire premise of his Islam was and is based on the Semitic doctrine of Revelation. As a point of clarification, although nowadays people use the word "Semite" to mean Jewish, in reality, Arabs also are Semites, as well as Sumerians, Caledonians, Babylonians together with a host of other people. The Iskamic principle that sovereignty belongs to Allah and must be conducted

according to his law is an extension of this Semetic
doctrine, and this is the source of all the problems that
followed.

Mohammad knew that Arabs could only be lifted to
a higher social level through his religion if the Jews would
also accept his religion and act as Arabs. Failing that, he
concluded that the Jews had to be made subservient to the
Arabs or be banished. In the Koran (Chapter 4, Verse 125),
he started with saying that:

وَمَنْ أَحْسَنُ دِينًا مِمَّنْ أَسْلَمَ وَجْهَهُ لِلَّهِ وَهُوَ مُحْسِنٌ ۞
وَاتَّبَعَ مِلَّةَ إِبْرَاهِيمَ حَنِيفًا وَاتَّخَذَ اللَّهُ إِبْرَاهِيمَ خَلِيلًا

*"Who can be better in religion than one who
submits his whole self to God, does good, and follows the
way of Abraham the true in faith? For God did take
Abraham for a friend."*

And in Chapter 2 Mohammad tried again to gain the
support of the Jews and have them accept his religion by
quoting from Allah that states: *"We made covenant with*
quoting from Allah: *"We made covenant with Abraham
and Esmail."* It did not work. The Jews did not bite the
bait.

We shall begin with the essential and elementary
groundbreaking decisions and will follow the development
of the system as closely as possible.

Financing a Movement

Mohammad's success was not accidental. He planned it carefully and enacted his plan diligently. He needed funds and men. Men would not come without funds. So, he put together an oligarchy that would provide the needed seed money and that in turn would bring in the needed funds.

Mohammad's plans were so tight and so controllable that no one other than a member of the Ghoreysh tribe could penetrate. The entire chain of command begins with Arabs being the best of the people on Earth the Ghoreysh being the best of the Arabs; Hashemis being the best of the Ghoreysh, and finally Mohammad being the best of the Hashemis who every Muslim has to follow and imitate. [Ends up in the establishment of the foundation of Islam.]

The Ghoreyshi Family Tree on the opposite page, (Page 51) depicts the significant personalities of the Ghoreysh tribe who were involved in the creation of Islam and the Arabic/Islamic Empire. Tracing the predecessors of the family, supposedly leads to Esmail (son of Abraham) and countinuing down the influential branches will lead to the ruling Arab dynasties that ruled the Islamic Empires for centuries. It is interesting to note that all of these ruling dynasties were of the Ghoreysh tribe.

Ghoreysh Family Tree

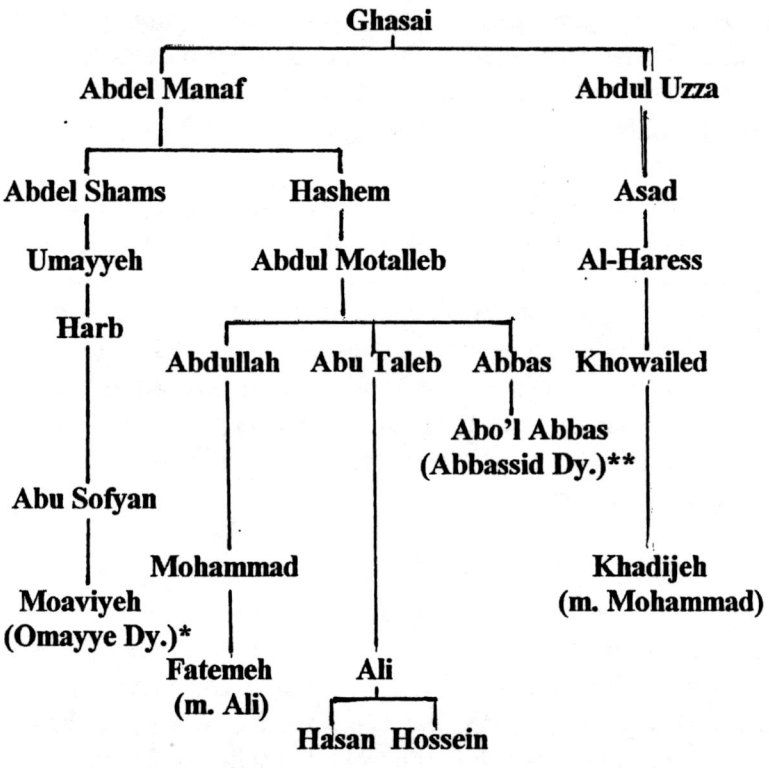

*   Progenitor of Amavid Dynasty
**   Progenitor of Abbasid Dynasty

Note: There were more and non-essential people involved than presented in this chart. The rest have been omitted due to lack of space.

Mohammad Creates
An Oligarchy of Sorts

The multitudes that followed Mohammad and made his movement a success had to be paid. As was mentioned in Book 1, Mohammad was financially poor and destitute, but otherwise he was mentally well endowed. To pay for services of those who followed him, he first married Khadijeh, a rich widow and one from Mecca's Ghoreysh noble class. Her money provided the initial funds needed for a major national movement.

Mohammad later married Aysheh, the six-year-old daughter of Abu Bakr, another nobleman of Mecca, who was rich, famous, combative, and who had connections. This marriage established family ties between the two, and put Abu Bakr's fortune at Mohammad's disposal and provided Mohammad with supporters and decisive military leadership. In return, Abu Bakr received the title al-Seddigh (the truthful one) and was appointed mayor of various cities. After Mohammad's death, he was elected as the first Khalifeh (Caliph).

Mohammad also married Hafsa, daughter of Omar ebn-Khattab, another opponent with power and connection. Omar distinguished his military career with his courage, and was noted for playing decisive roles in combat. He also was given the title Farough (the separator of right from wrong).

To strengthen his camp, Mohammad gave his two daughters in marriage to Ossman. First was Roghiyeh, who soon died from Ossman's severe beating – he was in the habit of horsewhipping, punching and kicking her. Then it was Omm Kolsum's turn, and Mohammad bestowed Ossman with the title Zolnoureyn (the twin-lights), in recognition of his abilities as a superb planner, administrator, and organizer of people of means.

Ossman brought in the nobles of Bani-Ommayeh who carried wealth and power of their tribe. It is said that Mohammad had told his friends that if he had another daughter he would have given her to Ossman also. The day Ossman was killed he had one hundred thousand Dinnars (gold coins) and one million Derhams (unit of money) in liquid assets, and the rest of his wealth in horses, camels, real estate holdings and farmland which was worth 200,000 Dinnars ($9.56 million). He was one of the Kateb-ol-Vahy (recorder of revelations) and a very close adviser and confidant of Mohammad. He was made mayor of Mecca and governor of various provinces time and again.

Mohammad had given his daughter Fatemeh to Ali (his cousin) in marriage. In the beginning, Ali was as poor and destitute as Mohammad, but after all the wars and consequent plunders, he died a very rich man, The attributes he brought to the camp were remarkable. He was a fearless fighter, a merciless killer, a faithful follower, an obedient server, and one who always used trickery when his physical power failed to accomplish the task. He claimed that he delivered and installed Islamic Ideology with the sword. His sword, with which he beheaded tens of thousands of men, was called Zulfaghar (two tipped). It is still on display in the Topkapi museum in Istanbul, Turkey.

He became the fourth Khalifeh, and he had become very rich by the time he was assassinated. In the township on Yanbaa alone his annual income from his date-palm orchards had been $0.5 million. Accounts of his wealth and numerous give-aways are too exaggerated to be mentioned in this book.

Zobair ben-Awam, another early convert to Islam, was not one of richest people in Arabia. The price of one of his inherited properties was estimated to be 50,000 gold Dinnars. He had 1000 male slaves, 1000 Kaniz (female slaves), and 1000 horses. In Medina he had eleven houses and many other properties in Basra, Kuffeh and Eskandarieh. Zobair was Mohammad's cousin (son of Mohammad's father's sister).

Alongside the members of his oligarchy, Mohammad had secured the financial support of the following wealthy nobles:

1. Abol-Rahman ben-Ouf, one of the richest nobles of Mecca and supporter of Mohammad. It is recorded that he had 1000 camels, 1000 horses, 10,000 sheep, and 5000 slaves. One-quarter of his inheritance was estimated to be worth $3.15 million, which means the entire inheritance was over $12.6 million (Please take these figures with several grains of salt. Arabia does not have enough annual precipitation to support so many slaves and livestock. Middle-Eastern reports, in general, and Islamic reports in particular are greatly exaggerated).

2. Talheh, a merchant whose daily income from his Mesopotamian grain fields alone was one thousand gold Dinnars. In addition, his wheat and barley were worth even more. For the bravery he showed in the Battle of Ohod, Mohammad promised him entry to the Islamic Paradise.

3. Zeyd ben-Sabet was one of Mohammad's closest advisers as well as one of the recorders of the Koranic Verses. When he died he had so many gold and silver bullions that axes were needed to divide them among the heir apparent. In addition to the bullions, he left 100,000 gold Dinnars ($4,78 million).

4. Khaled ben-Valid, was one of the richest nobles of the Ghoreush. Mohammad made him the commander of his cavalry. He received the title of Seyf-Ollah (Sword of Allah) for all the wars that he fought in behalf of Allah and His Messenger. Concerning his humanist values it should be noted that one night when he was the dinner guest of Malek ben-Moveryeh (a famous Muslim), he took his host by surprise and killed him, threw his severed head in the oven, and that same night copulated with the dead-man's wife. Abu Bakr, the First Khalife, having full knowledge of his character and the value he attached to his services to Islam, refused to punish him for his hideous crime.

   To obtain the support of wealthy and influential Arabs, Mohammad offered them protection against plunder, titles, women, more money, subjects, young beautiful boys, governorships, commands, and anything and everything to make his move a success.   He had promised protection for the wealthy and titles for the nobility.   When they supported him with wealth and fighters, Mohammad kept his promise.

The Situation of Islam
At the Time of Mohammad's Death

"God chose as the best the children of Esmail, the son of Abraham. From Esmail's descendants, God chose the Ghoreysh (the tribe of Mohammad) as the best of the people; from the Ghoreysh, God chose the Ban-Hashem (Mohammad's clan) as the best of the people, and from the Bani-Hashem, God chose Mohammad as the best of all the men..." (Al-Tirmidhi, Volune 2). Thus, Mohammad is designated as the best of men, and is to be imitated by all Muslims as a role model.

Jews are the descendants of Isaac. They believe that he was the only legitimate son of Abraham, born of his wife Sarah. Esmail was given birth by Hagar, an Egyptian maid, servant of Sarah, made pregnant by Abraham. Jews insist that according to the Torah, God made His covenant with Isaac and not Esmail.

Mohammad gave the children of Esmail (the Arabs) preference over the Jews. This action by Mohammad turned out to be a nationalistic act. The aftermath of this distinction is the foundation of the present-day conflict between Jews and Arabs. Each group claims to be the rightful heir to Abraham and the party to the covenant with Jehovah or Allah, and each refers to its Holy Book, given to them by the same Deity that, in this case, has two different names, along with many other names.

By and by Mohammad had elevated his status with respect to Allah. In the beginning he was the servant of

Allah. Then he became His Messenger at large. Later he was the person who, on the day of resurrection, would be standing at Allah's right side and who would bear witness for the believers (Al-Tirmidi, Volume 2). Ultimately, he elevated himself to the point where Allah and His angels pray to him and send him their salutations and greetings.

As was mentioned in Book 1, the Koran was not assembled into a book during Mohammad's life. It was Ossman, the third Khalife, who gathered the scattered Verses, eliminated some, and assembled the rest into a book that is now known as the Koran. What is referred as Shariat (Shari'sh) (the Law) is contained in the Koran. However, Islam is not conducted and Muslims are not governed by the Shariat alone. There are the Hadisses (Hadiths) (Discourse, Tradition) and the Sunnats (Traditions, Customs). They were recorded long after Mohammad's death. We list the names of the people who recorded them in the bibliography.

Mohammad died on the ninth day of June 632 A.D. He had neither organized nor established anything resembling what we nowadays would think of as a government. In the last ten years of his life he had established an army and ran a totalitarian regime by decree. To finance his army (governing structure) there were no taxes (public support) to be collected from the people who had nothing to give anyway. The army fought, conquered, plundered, enslaved and sold the enslaved defeated people, gave 20% of the loot to Mohammad, and kept the rest as its share. It should be noted that this 20% was not all that Mohammad received. The most beautiful women, the best of the horses and the most expensive of the jewelry were his also.

Later this 20%, after Mohammad's death, became part of the Islamic tax law and is referred to as Khoms. Khoms in Arabic means one fifth., hence 20%. However, both Shiites and Sunnis pay Zakat (tax). Islamic taxation will be covered separately. Nowadays, in Iran, it is referred to as "Sahme Emam," which means **(leader's share).**

Mohammad's decrees were of three kinds. There were (1) carried-over pagan Arab rights, (2) orders that Mohammad issued that were sure to be carried out, and finally (3) orders for which Mohammad had to invoke divine intervention. Through Archangel Gabriel, who had became an intermediary between him and his imaginary God "Allah," he produced the needed others in the form of Verses of the Koran. The latter left no room for question or disobedience.

His ever-obedient army was composed of Bedouin militiamen who assembled whenever Mohammad needed them. They had no logistics and no regular pay per se. Their pay was 80% of the loot including material possessions such as gold, silver, land and animals, in addition to enslaved women and children. The old and young men were usually either killed or sold into slavery. Pretty young boys were kept for carnal use and as household servants. This army lived on the spoils of wars.

The spoils of wars were not the only motivating forces for these Bedouin fighters. Women and pretty

young boys, both here on earth and later in the promised
Islamic Paradise, were equally valued. The women that
they captured were not enough – Mohammad promised
them 72 ever-virgins in Paradise. They are called Houri,
and their beauty was well described. As far as Mohammad
was concerned, every Arab was a potential soldier.

Mohammad had told the desert wanderers that there
was not much on this Earth for them – which they so well
knew. He taught them that the real and everlasting life
begins in Paradise. All they had to do was get themselves
into Paradise. Mohammad had convinced them that he was
the only one who could vouch for them in front of Allah.
The proposition was very simple. Come and fight for Allah
and me. If we win you get 80% of the loot plus entry into
the promised Paradise, and I get the remaining 20%. If you
die, you go directly to Paradise. The minute you arrive in
Paradise you get 72 ever-virgin Houris. A man's masculine
virility will be increased hundredfold. His physical body
would be restored to its prime condition of thirty years of
age and will stay as such forever. Life in Paradise is
eternal. There is a river of wine, a river of honey, a river of
milk, fruit trees, 72 Houris, and as many Ghelmans as they
please. Ghelmans are the young pretty boys who will serve
in any way you please. Description of the Islamic Paradise
and the Islamic Hell will be presented in a separate book.

Mohammad was not the only Arab to claim to be a
prophet. Taliha, chief of the Bani Asad tribe, also made the
claim, but was defeated by Khalid ben-Valid. There was
also Musleimeh the Kazzab (the liar) who worked miracles.
He was killed in the battle of Al-Yaman. Another claimant

was Al-Aswad (the Veiled Prophet) of Yemen who was eliminated by Muslims. And there was a woman called Sajjah, daughter of Haress eebn-Soveyd, who, after the death of Mohammad, claimed to have received revelations from Heaven. The Tribe of Hazil accepted her claim, and their chiefs agreed to fight alongside her against Abu Bakr.

Wars between Muslims and those who had abandoned Islam and gone back to their old ways, or had joined another proclaiming prophet littered the pages of Arabian history during the reign of the four Khaliphehs.

Mohammad succeeded where others had failed, because, unlike the others, he was a superb politician, a shrewd planner, a first-class nationalist, and a superb orator. Had he not won the support of Omar and Abu Bakr, he too would most likely have failed.

By the way, Abu Bakr (or Abu Kekr) means **the father of the virgin.** Indeed he was the father of the seven-year-old virgin girl called Aysheh who became Mohammad's child-bride at that age. No man had known her before her marriage to Mohammad at the tender childish age of seven, and that marriage was not consummated until she became of age when she was nine. On the basis of this act of Mohammad, in Islam a girl is ready for marriage when she turns nine.

Perhaps his most effective attributes was his sense of nationalism. He advocated monotheism, yet he adapted centuries' old pagan Arab rituals. The Hajj and its relayed ceremonies had existed long before him; he did not reject them. Most of the ceremonies are superstitious acts, and he adapted them for Islam. Allah had been an old idol worshipped by the Ghoreysh. Mohammad elevated it to be the God of Islam. Initially he had named Jerusalem as the Ghebleh (Kiblah)(direction of prayer) of the Muslims in the hope that he would attract the Jews, but, after sixteen months, he declared Kaaba as the Ghebleh of the Muslims. Hadiss 5903 (Muslims) suggests that Omar was the instigator of this change.

Mohammad promised not only the Paradise to the Muslim Arabs but homage to be paid to them by all the Muslims of the world. To be a good Muslim one had to perform three specific acts: First, recite the Touhid (Bear witness that there is no other God but Allah). Second, recite the Nabovvat (Bear witness that Mohammad is the Messenger of Allah). Third, recite the Maad (Declaration of one's belief that there will be a Day of Resurection). These three together constitute the three Pillars of the Faith. Both the Sunnis and the Shiites are in agreement on these three essential duties. However, the Shiites have added two more duties to the three basics: the Adelleh (the evidence of proof) and the Emamat (the succession of Imams).

In addition to those three duties for the Sunnis – or five for the Shiites – there are several good recommendations (to-do acts), which are not duties. Those include praying five times each day while facing the Ghebleh (Kaaba), fasting one month of the year in the month of Ramazan (Ramadan), and finally, make the pilgrimage to Mecca at least once in a lifetime, provided that one can afford to do so.

Let us begin with the first and foremost of the duties, the **Touhid**, which is the Arabic word for "declaration of oneness." The meaning is to bear witness that there are no other gods but Allah. Without Allah, Islam cannot and does not exist.

The second duty (must) is the **Nabovvat**, which means "prophetic mission." Again, without acknowledgement that Mohammad is the Messenger of Allah, Islam cannot and does not exist.

The third is the **Maad**, which means "future life or resurrection," or in other words, acknowledging one's belief that there will be a Day of Resurrection and Judgment. Without that, Islam cannot be enforced and will not be worth the trouble.

Where the Shiites are concerned, there is a fourth duty and it is called **Adelleh**. It means the *"evidence or proof"* for the aforementioned three. The Sunnis do not accept this belief.

For the Shiites there is also a fifth duty, without which Shiites cannot exist, and that is called **Emamat**. By believing in emamat they confirm their "belief in Imams." Without Imams Shiites would be Sunnis.

Among the recommendations are several that are almost as strong as duties. Every Muslim does them faithfully, as faithfully as breathing. One would almost think that they would die if they didn't.

Let us begin with the daily prayers. One prostrates himself five times each day toward the   Mecca. That is not as simple as it sounds. Consider all of the Muslims all over the world and in different time zones, with over one billion Muslims prostrating toward Mecca, it means that there is not a single moment in a day that large groups of people are not bowing toward Mecca in unison. Here it is not Allah that is essential, it is the Ghebleh – Mecca -- that they bow to. They all bow toward the Ghebleh, and they all know that they are not alone in the performance of this ritual, for millions of others, all over the world, are bowing to the same Ghebleh at the same time and in the same way.

Then there is the holy month of Ramazan when all Muslims fast. It is another practice that offers a daily discipline and provides a sense of unity and belonging. At the present time, in the twenty-eight-day of the lunar month, over one billion Muslims all over the world engage in the practice and are mindful of the unity of the Islamic world. It is indeed a very powerful reminder of their unity, because over one billion Muslims are going through the same bodily deprivation at the same time.

Hajj is the cornerstone of the system that assures the survival of Arabs. Yet, Hajj is not the only pilgrimage made by the Muslims to Arabia. There is another pilgrimage known as Umreh Ceremonies that attracts just about as many pilgrims as Hajj does. The only difference between Hajj and Umreh is that Hajj takes place in the Arabic lunar month of Zihajjeh and includes the Festival of Ghorban (Sacrifice); however a pilgrimage made at any other time of the year is called Umreh.

Each year over two million pilgrims converge on and congregate in Mecca. The cost of this pilgrimage, nowadays, is about $5000 per person. Considering that there are a minimum of two million pilgrims for the Hajj alone, the cash flow into Arabia is over ten billion dollars per annum. The population of Arabia is about 20 million. Thus, Hajj provides an annual average **per capita** income of about $500. That has been going on for the last fourteen centuries. Estimating the dollar figure can only establish a present-day criterion of cash flow, but level of income has been at a comparative level for the last fourteen centuries. Umreh Ceremonies attracts as many pilgrims and produces as much income for the Arabs as does the Hajj. Mohammad established an everlasting source of income for his nation. He was a first-class and devoted nationalist indeed.

Allah had indicated His reasons for the creation of Man. In Chapter 2 He says *"I have not created man except to serve me."* In return for all the services He provides for Mohammad; all He craves is love and worship. Allah loves to be glorified all the time. It is interesting to note that He is never glorified without Mohammad. Toward the end of Mohammad's life, Allah and His angels end up praising and greeting Mohammad.

When Mohammad returned from Hajj-ol-Vadaa (the last Hajj) the symptoms of a deadly disease were visible. Apparently he had not planned for what was to be done after his death – no plans for the distribution of his wealth or for a successor. There was no written will and no procedure to be followed.

What he left behind was an Arabia that was under one command. All those who opposed him, and some who had even put a price on his head, had either surrendered to Mohammad and accepted Islam, or like Atiba, Shaiba and Abu Jahl had died in battles against Mohammad. It is interesting to note the terminology that is used in this connection. Those who surrendered survived. The word Islam means "Surrender," a total and complete surrender of everything. The worst part of this submission is for a person to surrender his individuality, his national identity, and his right to think, to reason, and to decide.

Among his archenemies were Abu Sofian, who was nullified by being appointed the Governor of Najran in Southern Arabia, and Khaled ben-Valid, who was appointed as the commander of a large portion of the Islamic Army.

Mohammad, with the help of three accomplices, had made his first attack on a Mecca bound caravan. A mere nine years later, at the end of his life, when he sent his last expedition to Syria, he had amassed thirty thousand fighters who had ten thousand horses.

Like kings, Mohammad wanted to send delegates to the courts of neighboring countries and receive their ambassadors. For that purpose he named the ninth year of Hijrat Amm-ol-Vfud, to mean the year of reception of foreign delegates. The Charge de Affairs of Mohammad was Balal, who was from Abyssinia, and who would receive delegates from various Arab tribes at Ramle Ben Haress in the Najarrieh district.

A high-ranking Christian clergyman from Najran in the Southern Arabia (population of Najran was mostly Christian) came to visit Mohammad and ask his permission for the Christians to practice their religion. Mohammad brought Verse 28, Chapter IX;

$$\text{(٢٨) يَـٰٓأَيُّهَا ٱلَّذِينَ ءَامَنُوٓاْ إِنَّمَا ٱلْمُشْرِكُونَ}$$

$$\text{نَجَسٌ فَلَا يَقْرَبُواْ ٱلْمَسْجِدَ ٱلْحَرَامَ بَعْدَ}$$

$$\text{عَامِهِمْ هَـٰذَا ۚ وَإِنْ خِفْتُمْ عَيْلَةً فَسَوْفَ}$$

$$\text{يُغْنِيكُمُ ٱللَّهُ مِن فَضْلِهِۦٓ إِن شَآءَ}$$

$$\text{إِنَّ ٱللَّهَ عَلِيمٌ حَكِيمٌ}$$

"O ye who believe! Truly The Pagans are unclean; so let them not, after this year of theirs, approach the Sacred Mosque. And if ye fear poverty, soon will Allah enrich you. If He wills, out of His bounty. For Allah is all-knowing, all-wise."

The second half of the verse has to do with the Arabs who had to leave their occupation for daily prayers and thus not engage in their business.

Upon return from Mecca, Mohammad dispatched a military expedition to Syria headed by Assameh, son of his adopted son Zayd. Immediately after this order Mohammad fell sick and soon passed away. His illness started with high fever together with extreme pain in his back and stomach, such that he could not go to the mosque for prayer. He sent Abu Bakr in his stead. Some claim that he was poisoned by one of his wives.

Assameh had not reached Syria by the time Mohammad passed away, so he returned to Medina immediately. Ali, Abol-Fazl son of Abbas (Mohammad's cousin), Ossameh ebn-Haress, Shokran (the freed slave of Mohammad), Uss ebn-Khouli, Aysheh, and other wives of Mohammad were present at his death-bed. Since Mohammad had not chosen a successor, Abu Bakr, Omar, and Ali sat in a session to decide what to do. Abu Bakr was sixty years old and was respected by most of the Muslims, whereas Ali was a brash 33-year-old man with no experience to deal with Abu Bakr. While the Muslims were in disarray and mourning, Omar pulled his sword and screamed "Why are you crying? Mohammad, our prophet, has not died! He has ascended to the Heaven next to Allah, and shall return shortly! Should anyone exclaim that the prophet is dead, I shall sever his head!"

Abu Bakr calmed Omar down and turned to the audience and said, "Mohammad always said that he is a mortal, like you and me, and even though he might be a prophet, every mortal dies as others have done before."

In Saqife Bani Saedeh where Muslims had gathered, the situation was so bad that there could easily have been bloodshed. To prevent this, Omar approached Abu Bakr and pledged allegiance (Beyaat) to him. This changed the mood, and one by one Muslims came forth and pledged allegience to Abu Bakr. Thus, on June 8, 632, Abu Bakr was elected to succeed Mohammad as Khalifat rasul-Allah (successor to the Messenger of Allah).

The Beginning of a new Era
The Four Orthodox Khalifehs

What took place immediately after the death of Mohammad is of paramount importance because it laid the foundation for the future of Islam, and set the direction for the flow of upcoming events. If it were not for these four orthodox successors, Islam as we know it would not have survived.

Abu Bakr (573-634), who was also known as as-Seddigh (the truthful one), was the first Muslim Khalifeh, and he ruled from 632 to 634. He was born in Mecca in the Taim clan of the Ghoreysh tribe. It is said that he was among the first male persons who embraced Islam. He was a merchant by trade and was with Mohammad from the beginning, before the latter claimed to be the Messenger of Allah. From 622 to 632 he was Mohammad's chief adviser. He had no permanent public function except overseeing and supervising the annual pilgrimage of those who flocked to Mecca and occasionally, when Mohammad was ill, substituting for Mohammad in leading the public in Friday prayers. At times Mohammad had asked him to lead the public in prayers and he – Mohammad – followed him.

Now Mohammad was dead, and Arab unity was about to fall apart. Many Arab chiefs declared themselves leader and tried to take command of the army, Abu Bakr's Khalafat was occupied with suppressing various uprisings. The only tribes that did not rebel were those residing around Mecca, Medina, and Taef. Abu Bakr had to kill very many rebels, defeat their armies, and subdue their uprisings before he could take full command of the union. His chief opponent was Musailemeh, who had declared himself a prophet. Musailemeh was killed in battle, in eastern Najd, in May of 633. This battle is a major event in Islamic History because of its excessive brutality and incredible carnage. While suppressing uprisings, Abu Bakr came to realize the true value of plunder, since there was no more Jewish wealth to be confiscated and Arabic wealth was protected by Mohammad's commitment. So he began to direct successful expeditions from Arabia to the Mesopotamia (today's Iraq, which was under the Persian rule) and Syria (under the Byzantine rule), until his death on August 23, 634. Abu Bakr, prior to his death, designated Omar ebn-al-Khattab as his successor.

Sir William Muir states that had the Muslims suffered a single blow at the time of Abu Bakr, there would not be Islam today. Abu Bakr divided Arabia into eleven provinces and provided each with a military force. He appointed Khaled ebn-Valid as the commander in chief of all forces. Khaled's first task was to suppress the uprising of Bani Tah and Bani Assad tribes, who had rebelled under the leadership of Talhe. Talhe had declared himself a prophet and was trying to usurp power from Abu Bakr. Abu Bakr's other campaign was against the tribe of Bani Tamim.

Omar ebn-al-Khattab (A.D. 586-644), the second Khalife of Muslims, was born in Mecca to a woman called Khashimeh, daughter of Hashem ebn-Hashem, who was a cousin of Abdollah ebn-**Abdolmotalleb** (father of

Mohammad). He was from the clan of Adi, tribe of
Ghoreysh. A family bond between Mohammad and Omar
was established by Mohammad marrying Omar's daughter,
Omm Kolsum.

In order to clarify some Arabic expressions for the
American reader, it should be stated that Arabs, most of the
time, refer to a person as the "son of so and so" or the
"mother or father of such and such." For example
Mohammad had one son named Qasem. So, Mohammad at
times, is referred to as Abu-al-Qasem Mohammad ebn-
Abdollah, meaning, Mohammad the father of Qasem the
son of Abdollah. "Omm," on the other hand, means the
"mother of," hence Omm Kolsum, one of Mohammad's
wives (daughter of Omar) is called Omm Kolsum because
she had a daughter called Kilsum.

Omar reigned from 634 to 644. Upon Mohammad's
death he was largely responsible for – and credited with –
mediating between people of Medina and Muslims to
accept Abu Bakr, a Meccan, as the head of the state. Abu
Bakr relied greatly on Omar, and nominated him to be his
successor.

Omar's first act as the second Khalifeh was to
remove Khaled ebn-Valid from his post as the commander
of the cavalry. Omar changed the Arabic calendar to begin
with Mohammad's escape from Mecca. He also created the
Beyt-ol-mal (house of goods), which functioned as kind of
a bank and good-will store. Those who had more than they
needed dropped off their excess, and those who did not
have enough would take what they needed. He was the

first Khalifeh to establish a policy for the administration of the newly conquered lands. He established both the government law as well as the legal practice of the judiciary law in the early stages of the Islamic Empire. Omar had no choice but to attack neighboring countries. Local Arabs and their riches were protected, and there was nothing else to plunder inside the peninsula. He is the first Khalifeh to carry the title of Amir-al-Momanin (The Commander of the Believers).

During his reign there was a great infighting when it was time to divide the loot. Most thought that he was favoring Talhe and Zobeir by giving them the largest shares. This premise of being paid by the plundered loot, at the time of Omar and beyond, overshadowed Mohammad's orders. Ethics and morality, if there were any, were set aside. It is interesting to note that Arabic language does not have a word for "ethics." Due to its lack, and in its stead, Arabs use the word "al-akhlaghat," which means behaviors. They would argue that behavior means ethics also, and the word "al-akhlaghat has many philosophical meanings. It encompasses them all, including ethics.

In the year 635 Damascus was conquered. Muslims took over Shaam (today's Syria). After Damascus the Muslim army moved north. Homs was put under siege, and it caved in. Latakia was next. In a battle that took place outside of the city citadel, people of the city were defeated and the Muslims massacred them. In 636 A.D. Jerusalem, the center of the Jewish faith, was conquered. After Jerusalem, Amro Ahs, Omar's commander, moved toward Egypt with 4000 Arabs. When the news of this move reached Omar, he immediately dispatched help; and with 15,000 under Amro's command, Egypt was conquered. Alexandria was next to fall.

The next prize for Omar to win was Iran. So far no one had dared to challenge the Sassanid Dynasty. Omar took the initiative, and Kaskar, al-Shbar, Kes al-Natef, Buyeb Halavan and Ghadesiyeh were the major battles that took place. Rostam Farrokhzad, courageous commander of Iranian Army, was killed by halal ben-Alghameh. Tisfoon, one of Sassanid capitals, which was within miles of today's Baghdad, fell to the Arab forces. This loss marked the beginning of the end of Sassanid Dynasty. History will neither forget nor forgive Iranian Deylam, the Iranian commander, who surrendered 4000 Iranian soldiers to the Arabs.

Yazdgerd III, the Iranian king at the time, decided to face the Arabs once and for all. He assembled an army of 150,000 and faced the 60,000-80,000-strong Arab army in Jelola and then in Nahavand. With Arab trickery Iranian forces came out of the citadel of Nahavand and were taken by surprise. Iranians lost over 100,000 men, as well as the battle. Yazdgerd III died in 625 A.D. in Marve, and with his death the Sassanid Dynasty came to an end. He was 34 years old. He was the last of many great Iranian kings of several dynasties of the Persian Empire that had ruled the Greater Iran for several centuries.

As of that day Iran went under a dark cloud of submissiveness, superstitions, ignorance, fear, lack of national identity, loss of national pride, loss of freedom of mind, thought, speech, action and innovation. This dark cloud is still covering Iran, governing the minds of each Muslim Iranian through an indescribably mesmerizing fear. Iranian recognize this mind control mechanism and have given it several names, among them are "Davalpa" and "Bakhtak". Iran was not the only great power to fall to Arab invasion and suffer losses. Egypt suffered more and lost more than Iran did.

What befell Iran and Egypt, the two fabulous empires of the time, will be presented in separate books. Human history has never before and never since witnessed such an extensive and thorough assimilation. Egypt's loss was much greater and worse than the loss suffered by Iran. Egyptians lost everything – their language, their religions, their national identity, their culture, and their history. They became Arabs.

Omar's monstrosities committed in Iran were so horrible that Iranians, to this day, burn him in effigy every year on his day of death. He was finally attacked and fatally wounded by an Iranian called Firuz, alias Abu-Lolo, and he passed away a few days later, in the 23rd year of Hijrat (567 AS.D.). Before his death he designated Abdol-Rahman as his successor. However Abdol-Rahman declined the appointment, and Muslims elected Ossman as their leader and head of the state.

The procedure designed by Omar for the election, after Abdol-Rahmans's declination, is very interesting indeed. He declared that six persons should form the election committee. These six persons were to form a conclave (shoura) and confer for three days, and on the fourth day they were to elect the successor. These six men were: Talheh, Zabir, Ali, Abdol-Rahman ebn-Ouf, Saad ebn-abi-Vaqass, and Ossman ebn-Affan. Omar had ordered that 50 fighters, with drawn swords, should stand guard at the entrance of the conference place. They had orders to kill all six if election was not concluded as ordered. Ossman was elected.

Ossman (Othman or Uthman) ebn-Affan (576-656 A.D.), the third Muslim Khalifeh, regned from 644 to 656. He was born in Mecca, in the clan of AbShams or Omayye, tribe of Ghoreysh. He had married Mohammad's daughter Roghiyeh, who died as a result of his assault and battery. Mohammad replaced her with another daughter of his, Omm Kolsum. Ossman was already wealthy, and after joining the oligarchy became much wealthier from his share of the plunders of wars that he participated in.

Ossman carried the policies laid down by Omar. The conquests continued in east and west, and he raided the Byzantine Empire in the north. With the help of fleets organized in Syria and Alexandria, the Byzantines were defeated at sea and Cyprus was occupied. By 650, when the conquests were slowing down and the military expeditions were becoming less profitable, the social malaise that followed the rapid expansion from a small state to an empire became evident as an unavoidable aftermath. Military discipline and bureaucratic administration became irksome to the desert wanderers. Ossman was accused of nepotism, for appointing people from Bani-Omayyeh (his own clan) to governorships and other sensitive posts. Among his appointments from Bani-Omayyeh to high offices were Valid ebn-Aqbeh as governor of Kufe; and Marvan ebn-Hekam, Hokm ebn-abi-al Ahs, and Moavieh ebn-abi-Sofyan as commanders. Although they may have been appointed due to their efficiency, nevertheless, it was Ossman's way of distributing wealth and power among relatives.

All of the above-mentioned appointees had extensive criminal records of carnage, plunder and lawlessness. Every one of them had accumulated untold and incredible wealth.

Ossman's arrangement of a standard text of the Koran proved to be another cause for criticism. Troops in Egypt and Iraq mutinied. Mutineers from Egypt besieged Ossman in his house in Mecca. He not only received no help from the people of Medina, but because of all his plunders, they conspired to kill him. Co-conspirators were Ali, Abu-Zar, Emar ben-Yaas, Zeyd, Sahsah ben-Hatam, Maalek Ashtar and Adi ben-Hatam. Later, Aysheh (Mohammad's wife) and Talheh and Zobeyr also joined the group of conspirators. They were so revengeful that they even refused water to the besieged Ossman and his household. Onlu Ali broke rank and delivered water. The siege lasted two months. Finally one of Ossman's neighbors opened a passage from his house to Ossman's compound. A man called Mohammad ben-abi-Bekr, with the help of some friends, assaulted Ossman and killed him on June 17, 656. He was 82 years old.

Omar's body lay on the ground for three days, and

no one was willing to bury it. Ali came and took the body
to Baghii (Muslim graveyard) for burial, but people would
not allow it. Finally they had to bury it in Hash Koukab, a
Jewish graveyard.

During the reign of Ossman trouble flourished
everywhere. Muslims conquered Khorasan, a vast territory
in the north-east of Iran. Wherever they went they did
nothing but kill and plunder, enslaved thousands of women
and children, and used human blood to turn the watermills.

Ali ebn-abi-Taleb (600-661 A.D.), the fourth
Khalifeh of the Muslims, succeeded Ossman. Ali was
Mohammad's cousin and son-in-law. Ali's father, Abu-
Talib, was Mohammad's uncle (father's brother) and for a
short while was the chief of the clan of Hashem of the tribe
of Ghoreysh in Mecca. Ali grew up in Mohammad's
household; and as a boy when Islam was proclaimed he
was one of the first ones to become a Muslim. After Hijrat
(Mohammad's escape to Medina in 622 A.D.) he married
Mohammad's daughter Fatmeh (Fatimah), who bore him
two sons, Hasan and Hosein. He was a brave and ferocious
fighter and took part in nearly all of Mohammad's
expeditions and battles. He led an expedition to Yemen in
632, but other than that he never became a part of the elite,
either in Mohammad's lifetime or during the reign of the
first three Khilefehs.

On the day that Ossman was assassinated, in June
656, the Muslims of Medina recognized Ali as the fourth
Khalifeh. Three groups opposed Ali. One group was
called Nakessin, who made a pact (beyaat) with Ali but

then reneged on it. Talhe and Ubeyr were among the members of this group. Another group was called Qasedin, which included the Moavieh and his followers. Finally there were the Mareqin, composed of those who left Ali in the war of Saffein and became known as al-Khavarej (the outsiders). Talheh and al-Zubayr, along with Ayshe, daughter of Abu Bakr and widow of Mohammad, organized an armed opposition and engaged in a bloody battle that lasted seven days. This is known as the Battle of Jamal ("Jamal" means camel. The battle was so named because Ayshe was riding a camel during the fighting). In that battle Talheh and al-Zubayr were killed and Ayshe was taken prisoner.

The reasons for the ill will between Ayshe and Ali are well known to the Muslims. They date back to the episode of Saffvan, when Ayshe was left behind and a very handsome young Arab fighter picked her up. The two were absent from the camp for a long time. When they arrived Ali demanded that Mohammad should divorce Ayshe, and Mohammad declared her innocent by verses sent down to him by Allah through Gabriel. On top of this, there was the episode involving Zeynab, the wife of Zeyd, the adopted son of Mohammad. Upon observing her naked, Mohammad asked Zeyd to divorce her so that he could have her. Gabriel was used to bring the required verses from Allah and justify Mohammad's action and demand. Ayshe recognized that this was all a hoax, and that Mohammad was creating verses as he pleased to suit the situation and rescue him from unpleasant situations.

Gabriel's relationship with Mohammad should not

be taken lightly. At times he acted as wireless-transmission medium between Allah and Mohammad. At other times he was a pimp for Mohammad.   At still other times he scheduled Mohammad's copulations and dispatched Mohammad to perform his carnal duties with his various wives. He also used to assemble armies of angels to rain stones on Mohammad's enemies. He was a multitalented angel indeed.

Another opponent of Ali was Moavieh, the governor of Syria. He was seeking vengeance for his kinsman Ossman. Ali had not taken part in Ossman's assassination, but he had neither captured nor punished the assassins. So Moavieh held him responsible for lack of action. Moavieh led an expedition against Ali. An indecisive battle took place at Suffayn, south of Raqqe, near Basra. It was a long and bloody battle, with more than 90 encounters, with thousands of casualties on both sides. The decisive battle took place in Leylat ol-Harir where Moavieh's army was smashed. The commander of Ali's forces was in hot pursuit of Moavieh's fleeing forces when Moavieh summoned his experienced and sly counsel, Amro Ahs, conqueror of Egypt, and asked for his advice. Amro Ahis told him, "have your soldiers put the Koran on their spears and shout, 'We are all Muslims and should not fight each other.'"   Moavieh agreed. Ali's forces, seeing the Koran on top of spears and hearing the call for peace, stopped the fighting and both sides settled for arbitration.

The account of this arbitration is fascinating because it portrays the character of the Muslims who were running the show. It was agreed that both sides would accept the verdict. Moavieh appointed Amro Ahs, his sly counsel, as his representative, and Ali appointed Abu Musa Ashaari, who was an ignorant commoner. At the beginning of their negotiation Amro honored Aby Musa and paid him high respects, convinced him that the best way to resolve the conflict was to vote for the removal of both Ali and Moavieh. Abu Musa Ashari accepted the proposal, and Amro Ahs asked him to be the first to announce his decision because he was older. Abu Musa Ashaari accepted the honor bestowed on him for his age and made his declaration saying "O ye people, Amro Ahs and I have conferred with each other about your dilemma and have concurred that, in order to put an end to this conflict, it is befitting for us to dispose both Ali ebn-Abi-Taleb and Moavieh ebn-Abu-Sofyan from Khakafat and refer the election to you so that you may chose anyone you please for that office. Therefore, now, I am disposing Ali from his office." Then Amro Ahs took the stand and declared "O ye people, you have heard what Abu Musa said. He disposed Ali from his office, I too agree with him and do dispose Ali from his office, and I chose Moavieh ebn-Abu-Sofyan to be the Khalifeh of the Muslims. Moavieh is the nearest kin to Ossman and should be the one who succeeds him and to seek revenge for Ossman's blood."

Upon hearing this verdict, Ali's forces split in two groups. One group, who could not tolerate Ali's naivete, left him and became known as the Khavarej. They numbered about 20,000, and their leader was Masaar ben-Fadki. The second group remained faithful to Ali.

There was no further battle between the two forces.

However, Ali was disappointed and denounced the decision. Moavieh, on the other hand, was pleased. He took control of Egypt and launched raids of increasing severity against Iraq. Meanwhile Ali had to fight against the Khavarej, who opposed his policies. Even the annihilation of eight thousand Khavarej at Nahravan in July of 658 could not remedy his problems. Ali lost control of Khorasan (northeastern Iran) to local rebels in 659, and lost Hejaz in 660.

Ali's fortunes were declining. The massacre of Nahravan brought three Khavarej together: Abdol-Rahman ebn-Moljam Marvi, Barak ebn-Abdollah Tamimi, who convened in Mecca and decided that because Ali and Moavieh and Amro Ahs had created schism among Muslims, all three should die. The conspirators chose the 19th day of Ramazan to carry out their mission. In January of 661, Abdol-Rahman ebn-Moljam Marvi, in front of the Mosque of Kufe, attacked Ali with his poisoned sword and fatally wounded him. Two days later, on the 21st day of Ramazan, Ali passed away.

Barak ebn-Abdollah Tamimi, who was to ﻗﺘﻞ Moavieh, only succeeded in wounding him. The third assassin, Amro ebn-Barak Tamimi, who was assigned to kill Amro Ahs, mistook his target and killed Kharejat ebn-Khaddaqe instead.

Ali was so afraid that people might mutilate his lifeless body that he had asked to be buried at night in an unmarked grave. His supposed grave is near Kufe, where the new town of al-Najaf was built. The imaginary superhuman personality ascribed to Ali was supposedly passed on to his sons and descendants, who became known as Imams (leaders) and further clouded the superstitious atmosphere surrounding Shiism.

After Ali's death, Islam branched into two main and many subordinate sects, the two main ones being the Sunni and the Shiite. Shiism, although in minority, is the most important branch, and within it there are many other subordinate sects. Shiism might not have survived. But it not been for the killing of Hosein by Yazid, a bloody love story that we shall present separately. The Shiites made a national calamity out of a love rivalry between a very beautiful woman's husband and lover.

Ali's true life is covered in a Farsi book called *A Research In The Life Of Ali,* which hopefully will be translated into English and published for the benefit of the American public. The fantastic stories written about Ali and his descendants fill many books, and they are truly mind-boggling. Some consider him an incarnation of Allah, but even Allah cannot fit the picture.

Ali's real personality is shrouded in a huge mass of legend and superstition. He was basically a fearless, merciless, courageous and ferocious fighter, but by no means a gifted statesman. Iranians, in trying to free themselves from the Arab rule, chose Ali and his sons as their heros, and created legendary and unreal super-humans out of them. Unfortunately, their fictionalized entities came to have such a powerful presence that the original intent was lost, and the creator (Iranians) became slaves of their creation (shiism). Shiism is the end product of their creation, and it lives in and rules the minds of over 100 million Shiite Muslims.

Ali, like Mohammad, started as a poor boy, living in Mohammad's household. But like his master, he ended up rich.   Shiite clerics try to portray him as a very benevolent and poor fellow, who tied a stone to his stomach in order not to feel the pain of hunger, yet we should not overlook all the riches he plundered.   The annual income from only one of his palm-date orchards, in the city of Yanbo, was 40,000 gold Dinnars ($1.5 million). In the plunder of the city of Madaen, Ali took the largest share.   Historian Habib al-Seyr Khaneii wrote about the legendary riches that Ali took during these plunders.

There is a group of Muslims in Iran known as the Ali-Allahis. With no knowledge about the true character of Ali, they have elevated him to the level of Allah, and worship him as such.

About the crimes Ali committed in Iran, one should refer to the writings of prominent historians such as ebn-Balkhi, Ahmad ben-Balad Zari, Masuud ben-Abi-Yaghuh, and Dr. Abdol-Hosein Zarrinkub.

The Character of the
Arab Invasion Commanders

This subject will be presented in a separate book, but for now it is interesting to note in retrospect that, through brute force, people can be made to worship their executors. Muslim Iranians of the Shiite sect worship Ali and his descendants as much as they worship Allah – if not more. Here is a brief and partial account of what was done to the Iranians.

After the fall of the Sassanid Dynasty, people of Iran constantly and continuously fought against the conquerors and occupiers. Between the 28th and 30th year of Hijrat, after the fall of Estakhr (a Sassanid Capital), people of that city rebelled against the Arabs. Ossman was the Khalifeh at the time. He dispatched Abdollah ebn-Amer to subdue the rebellion. People's resistance was so fierce that ebn-Amer swore he would kill so many that their blood would turn the watermill's milling stone. He was true to his words. Over 40,000 people were killed, and to prevent their blood from clotting he ordered it to be diluted with water.

During the reign of Ali ebn-Abitaleb, the people of Estakhr again rebelled against the Arab invaders. Ali dispatched a close friend of Mohammad, Abdollah ebn-Abbas of the Bani-Hashem clan, to deal with the rebellion. Abdollah had been with them in previous wars and plunders. He drowned the rebels in Iranian blood.

Another Iranian city to fall to Ali's forces was Nishabur. By the time Ali conquered it, there were no more fighters left alive to resist.

Next was Ray's turn to fall victim to Ali's conquests. The people of Ray resisted until they could do so no more.

While the people of Estakhr were rebelling against Arabs, there were also uprisings in Kerman and Fars. Ali dispatched Zayd ben-Obeyd, another blood-thirsty commander, to quash the rebellion. This fellow was the out-of-wedlock son of Abu-Sofyan and half brother of Moavieh, whose mother, Samye, had the oldest profession in Taef. His acts will be covered in the book on Ali.

The Arabs have an expression concerning the Iranian people. "Three things passing in front of a mosque make a prayer worthless and unacceptable – first is an Iranian, second is an ass, and the third one is a dog."

The Iranians finally were successful in expelling Arabs from their country. But, unfortunately, all the pagan Arab traditions and social behavior remained in Iran in the format of Islam.

Conquering countries, suppressing and subjugating people, extinguishing the fires of rebellion and subduing uprisings are among the functions of the conquerors. But when a conquered nation begins to worship its conquerors the way it worships God of gods, there must have been something askew with the minds of the conquered people to begin with, or something horrible must have been done to their minds by those who conquered them.

Bibliography

Al-Zomokhshari.   *Al-Kashef al Haghighat al-Tanzil.*
     Published in Cairo. (Arabic)
Balazari. *Ftoot al-Baladan.* (Arabic)
Masuudi. *Marvaj al-Sabab.* (Arabic)
Koran. Elmi Publications, Published in Tehran, Iran.
Ali Dashti. 23 Years. Published in London. (Farsi)
Bijan Faghfur. *Mohammad, Prophet King of Arabs.*
     Kanoon Publications, Los Angeles. (Farsi)
Hassan Abbas. *From Mitra to Mohammad.* Homa
     Publications. (Farsi)
Ali Mir-Fetros. *Islamology.* Afra Publications, France.
     (Farsi)
Grishman. *Iran, From Start to Mohammad.* Translated by
     Dr. Moin. Published by Book Translation and
     Publishing Foundation, Tehran, Iran. (Farsi)
Dr. Roshangar. *Shiism and Mahdism.* Pars Publications,
     San Francisco. (Farsi)
Hamid Damghani. *Fars Name ebn-Balkhi.* Farahani
     Publications. Tehran. (Farsi)
Dr. Abdol-Hosein Zarrinkub. *Iranian History After Islam.*
     Amir Kabir Publications, Tehran. (Farsi)
Ahmad ebn-abi-Yaaghub. *Tarikh Yaaghubi.* (Farsi)
Bahram Chubine. *Tashayo va Siyasat.* (Farsi)
Khavandir. *Tarikh Habib-ol-Seyr.* (Farsi)
Gorgi Zidan. *Tarikh Tamadone Eslam.* (Farsi)
Edward Brown. *History of Iranain Literature._*Translated
     by Ali Pasha Saleh, Tehran University Publication.
Julius Welhousen. *The Religio-Political Factions in Early
     Islam.* North Hollan Publishing Co., 1975

William Muir. *The Life of Mohammad.* London-Luzac & Co., 1933

Dr. Roshangar. *Bazshenasiye Koran.* Pars Publications, San Francisco. (Farsi)

Encyclopedia of Religion and Ethics. James Hasting New York: Charles Scriben and Sons, 1921

Tarikh Tabari. Translated by Abol-Kasem Payandeh, Asatir Publications, Tehran. 1363. (Farsi)

Ebn Hashem. *Sirate Rasuk-Ollah.* Translated by Qazi Abar-Qoveh, Researched by Dr. Asghar Mahdavi. (Farsi)

Abdol-Azim Razii. *Tarikhe Duh-Hezar Saleye Iran.* Published in Iran. (Farsi)

Gen. Sir Purcy Saix. *History of Iran.* Translated by Seyyed Mohammad Taghi Fakh Daii Gilani. Published in Iran. (Farsi)

Seyyed Hashem Rasuli Mahalati. *Zendegiye Amir-al-Moumenin.* (Farsi)

Dr. Abol-Hosein Zarrinkub. *Do Qarn Skut.* (Farsi)

About the author

Armen A. Saginian is a registered professional mechanical engineer in the State of California and is listed in Who is Who in California 1983, Who is Who in the West 1987-88, and Who is Who in Hell 2000. Armen was born in Tabriz, Iran, February 2, 1933. He finished his elementary and secondary education in Iran and ca,e to the United States in 1955.

He attended Maryville college in Tennessee majoring in Mathematics 1955-1959, the University of Tennessee majoring in Mechanical Engineering 1959-1961, and Graduate School of Business Administration at UCLA 1968-1972.

Armen worked in the Aerospace industry from 1961-1975, went to Iran with his own project to bring electrical power, potable and irrigation water, schools, hospitals, public baths, cold storage, year[round farming, and light industry to 66,000 primitive villages, and bring them up to 20th century standards. The massive project was aborted because of the 1979 revolution in Iran that put all such projects on hold. He returned to the United States and worked on the Uranium Enrichment Project until 1985.

Armen retired from industrial work in 1985 and devoted the rest of his life to free the minds of the people that are enslaved by dogma and superstitions injected into them by the merchants of the craft (the clerics) whose aim is to create havoc and problems for the rest of the world.

VIOLENCE EMBEDED IN ISLAM

These articles written by Fatemolla, a pen name, are designed to inform the public in general, and the American public in particular about the intricacies of Islamic Law(s), the Shariat, that makes a Muslim act in a way that is not compatible with the Western culture and way of life.

A concept that is basic in the Western life and is referred to as Ethics does not exist in Islamic culture. Muslim scholars try to explain it away by stating that what they refer to as *Elm-ol-Akhlaq* is the same as Ethics. That is a false and misleading claim. Sure enough, when looking into English-Arabic dictionary, in front of Ethics it says Elm-ol-Akhlaq; however, looking for the English word in the Arabic-English dictionary, Elm-ol-Akhlaq is translated as **"behavior."**

Islamic behavior is governed by the **Shariat.** And Shariat does not parallel the Western Ethical Standards.

This book is published by:

New Horizons
P.O. Box 896
Glendale, CA 91209
www.cfiwest.org/newhorizons
e-mail: Armen@cfiwest.org
Tel. 323-666-4278, Fax. 323-666-4271

ROOTS OF TERROR IN ISLAM

Islamic apologists, as of September 11, 2001, have been playing the new tune that *"Islam is a religion of peace."* Nothing can be further from the truth. They may be some verses, copied from other religions, which do indeed talk about benevolence; however, Islam began with violence and is continuing with violence. Articles in this book are the writings of Syed Kamran Mirza, who used to be a Muslim. Syed Kamran Mirza is a pen name.

Islamic violence is not preached only in Islamic schools and Madrassas (religious schools) overseas. Right here in the United States, new Mosques open every year and new Islamic schools are established in various cities of the country that do just that, preach violence. All they teach is from the Koran and the Sharia. Read the verses in this book, which are taken from the Koran, and draw your own conclusion. Should anyone argue that they have been taken out of context, by all means take the entire Koran ans read it.

This book is published by:
New Horizons
P.O. Box 896
Glendale, CA 91209
www.cfiwest.org/newhorizons
e-mail: Armen@cfiwest.org
Tel. 323-666-4278, Fax. 323-666-4271

Islam, the Arab Imperialism
By Anwar Shaaikh

Muslims from all over the world are fearded as terrorists in the Western world. Is it propaganda or misunderstanding? It is neither. Frankly states, it is the truth.

Islam has divided humankind into two perpetually hostile groups, i.e., the Muslims and the non-Muslims. The former have the duty to hate their own fathers, mothers, brothers, sisters and countrymen if they practice a different faith. The Muslims must force the infidels to embrace Islam, using any means including murder, rape, looting, arson, deception, and treason.

Until a country has embraced Islam, it is legally considered a battlefield (Dar-ul-harb), and the Muslims are obliged to betray their own motherland through civil and military action. Once it is converted to the Muslim ideology, it ranks as a Land of Peace (Dar-us-Salam) but at a very high cost to one's national pride because then it exists as a spiritual and cultural satellite of Arabia. This is what makes Islam the subtle tool of Arab Imperialism.

Islamic ideology, which is based on intence hatred of the non-Muslims, is beginning to loom as Islamophobia in the West.

This bok is published by:

New Horizons
P.O. Box 896
Glendale, CA 91209
www.cfiwest.org/newhorizons
e-mail: Armen@cfiwest.org
Tel. 323-666-4278, Fax. 323-666-4271

Islam

The Arab National Movement

Most uninformed people consider Islam a religion, like any other religion. That is not so. Islam began as a movement, a national movement at that, in Arabia.

Islam began with Mohammad who was too smart to remain a camel herder or a poor desert wonderer. He was bright; he was handsome; he was courageous; and above all, he was ambitious.

Mohammad began with preaching monotheism, and soon found out that it does not work. He married a rich woman and continued preaching. His wife and uncle died, and he found out that he had to make a living for himself. He decided that he should unite the Arabs and rule them. Thus, he created an oligarchy and started the movement.

His life was not long enough to do more than what he accomplished in twenty-three years. But the movement continued after his death.

Anwar Shaikh has done a great job presenting this aspect of Islamic reality in his book that he calls *Islam, the Arab National Movement*.

This book is published by:

New Horizons
P.O. Box 896
Glendale, CA 91209
www.cfiwest.org/newhorizons
e-mail: Armen@cfiwest.org
tel.323-666-4278, Fax 323-666-4271

Islam, sex and violence

By: Anwar Shaikh

"Besides sex and violence, Islam seems to have a third approach, which is rational. It declares that there is 'no coercion in religion' (2:255) and the truth must be vindicated by proof (2:111). If the Muslim can prove that the contents and conclusions of this book are false or far-fetched, I shall be honor-bound to apologies publicly; otherwise they must hold their peace and rethink about the divine origin of Islam," so declares the author.

Seldom, if ever, has any author gone this route of investigation. This book is a must reading for one who is still bewildered by the recognition of Islam's true nature.

This book is published by:

New Horizons
P.O. Box 896
Glendale, CA 91209
www.cfiwet.org/newhorizons
e-mail: Armen@cfiwest.org
Tel. 323-666-4278, Fax 323-666-4271

In Search of True Islam!

Islamic apologists, nowadays, are hard pressed to explain their troubles away. The amount of money spent annually by the governments of Saudi Arabia, Iran, Libya and other Islamic countries is a huge sum, and contribution of the Iranian Government to this fund is over $100,000,000.00 one hundred million U.S. dollars.

Read this booklet and other booklets that portray the true Islam for you. Otherwise, if you choose to believe their propaganda, I know a person who is selling the Brooklyn Bridge and would like to talk to you.

This book is published by:

New Horizons
P.O. Box 896
Glendale, CA 91209
WWW.cfiwest.org/newhorizons
e-mail: Armen@cfiwest.org
Tel. 323-666-4278, Fax. 323-666-4271